CONTENTS

CONTENTS

ILLUSTRATIONS

ACKNOWLEDGEMENTS

I should like to thank especially Mr J. I. M. Stewart, the Revd. E. G. Midgley and Professor J. J. Lawlor. They have helped me perhaps more than they know, whether in what might be called the genesis of this book or in its writing. I am greatly indebted also to critics and writers on these subjects; so many are they that to name any one would be invidious.

Finally, grateful acknowledgement is due to the following for permission to use illustrations; The British Museum, The Bodleian Library, The National Gallery, The Boston Museum of Fine Arts, and British Lion Films: to Messrs Faber and Faber for permission to quote from the work of William Golding, and to Oxford University Press for allowing me to use C. W. Kennedy's translation of the Old English *Genesis*.

FOREWORD

'It takes at the best, I think, a great deal of courage and patience to live', Henry James wrote to a despondent friend. 'But one must do everything', he went on at once, 'to invent, to force open, that door of exit from mere immersion in one's own states.' James's own door of exit—he calls it cautiously 'a certain amount of remedy'—was into that sort of absorbed contemplation of the general human state which may have, as a farther door of exit, the release of imaginative creation. There are other farther doors, such as those opening upon religious convictions or speculative systems. And there are doors in the creating of which intellect and imagination have supremely coalesced, so that the resulting vision is like that of a man to whom it has been granted to stand for a time at the heart of a universe in which order everywhere declares itself amid the divine abundance. Dante's poem and Milton's are such doors as these.

As soon as we think we seek an architecture in things. For we survive or succeed only in the measure that we understand; we have to know why the bough trembles, the twig snaps, the wind carries this scent or that. Bewilderment is an enemy, and it remains alarming even when occasioned by the larger, the less immediately threatening situations to which our awareness reaches out. As we grow reflective it may even become the total spectacle of ourselves in our universe that is the most daunting fact of all. But we are not bewildered only; we take leave to be outraged as well. We are entitled, we feel, to a world that makes sense; to fortunes explicable in terms of a scheme of things echoing, with a reassuring familiarity, the devices and desires of our own hearts. We have been thwarted, frightened by the sheer recalcitrance and disregardingness of our environment; overtaxed by the unending task of keeping going. Have we not deserved better, we cry, than this bitter toil, these blighted hopes the final embrace of corruption and the worm? Surely it was not always so? Nobody deliberately fashions a shaky adze, a warped spear. *So what went wrong?*

We do not positively know that this question is unasked by apes; indeed, we may sometimes think to read its mute reflection in their eyes. But human history certainly does not begin until its shadow hangs over the minds of men, and it is itself a question that posits a historical sense; it cannot be asked except in terms of the idea of history, although the first prompting to it may have been through the contemplation of present disaster. Flood or fire or pestilence may drastically change for the worse the conditions of life here and now; it requires only a little command of thinking by analogy to speculate about some aboriginal calamity. We should today call such speculation rational, and cease to call it so as soon as it is infiltrated by animistic notions. As with the warped spear so with a deformed child, a hard winter, a barren soil. All are artefacts, but none could be fashioned so except as punishment or in malice. This thought, itself rational albeit perhaps with a false premise, must be among the most portentous ever achieved by man. Paradoxically, human dignity is born with it. Adam and Prometheus and Lear are stirring in the night of their forebeing. There is just one further tremendous step in the definition of man.

Again, perhaps, magic prompted it. If we are all at times tempted to be less well-conducted than the tribe would approve, does the explanation not lie in demonology? Are there demons which do not so much come and go as sleep and wake? Satan and the rebel angels, some psychologists tell us, inhabit a nether world which in fact consists of the buried strata of the developed human psyche. However this may be, we feel it as a fact that we may be betrayed by what is false within. Even what we have is threatened by what we are.

The problem of evil has arrived—of evil and of the sense of sin. We are at once responsible and not responsible for our own deteriorated condition. The contradiction, the mystery shows no sign of being other than too deep for us; it would be optimistic to suppose that it is ever going to be resolved. But there have been attempts. And childhood has appeared to some a hopeful point of attack. We would do well to consider our own childhood, or even perhaps a childhood of the race.

That act is wrong which we get slapped for if we are caught out as perpetrating it, and the slap is administered for the ease and convenience of persons stronger than ourselves. Guilt is a kind of dread, a fear of being found out. That men are thus disobedient children who have been detected, punished, and indoctrinated with a wholesome sense of disgrace or sin is an explanation of our present state so persuasive that we have nodded our heads in acquiescence to it for aeons, interwoven it with doctrines of the Fatherhood of a single omnipotent and beneficent God, or—stressing, as it were, its reductive possibilities—have exhibited it as strikingly consonant with one or another conjectural anthropology, and particularly with a development of moral feeling from notions of sexual transgression generated in the primeval social group or horde.

What we have in all this is a groping for intelligibility, and in particular for what can be felt as *universally* true. The story we want is the story of Everyman, because it is that story which, as we listen to it, most effectively lightens the burden of 'mere immersion' in our own states and brings us—but always and only if the *art* be powerful enough—'courage and patience to live'.

Hence the great aetiological myths—including that one central to the Western imagination which is the subject of Mr Smith's penetrating, subtle, and learned inquiry in this book. These stories set out to tell us—whether as historical fact divinely revealed and authenticated, or as allegory, or as fable, or as a cunning weft and web of these—*why it is* and *how it happened*. A few, and among them the fully evolved myth of the Fall of Man, attempt a larger synthesis. They tell us, too, *how it is going to end.* Modern treatments of the theme lack confidence here, are more convinced of our loss of innocence, our 'essential illness', than of any Redemption achieved or to come. When Simon in *Lord of the Flies* (the discussion of which Mr Smith has advanced very notably indeed) looks out over 'the divider, the barrier' of ocean and says to Ralph, 'You'll get back where you came from', his voice is that of one no longer commonly heard. It is not even, to my ear, quite William Golding's voice.

In this book, then, we watch masters of the human imagination grappling, over a period of more than a thousand years, with a haunting and transcendent theme. Each labours in terms of his own idiosyncratic vision—the idiosyncrasy yet being controlled by a multitude of affiliating bonds with tradition and with the preoccupations and persuasions of an age. It is an intricate history, and as he pursues it Mr Smith permits himself no hint of facile simplification. I believe his work will thus appeal alike to scholars and to all of us who have paused to think for a little after finishing any version of the Fall.

J. I. M. STEWART

INTRODUCTION

Like many a reader of *Paradise Lost* I have often approached this
vast work out of a sense of duty, read the first three or four Books
and skimmed the rest, or, sensing that by this procedure I cannot
have done full justice to the meat of the poem, I have started by
concentrating on the story of the human Fall in Books IX and X,
then expanded the canvas as time and interest dictated and read
back and forward, sampling the scenes in heaven and hell before,
and the visions of consequential events after, the scene to which
all is directed. Neither method has been satisfactory. Wherever
you start, you seem to become conscious of the pressure of what
you have not read. You compare one account of a situation with
another, one character with the comments of another character,
one level of style with another. Often you end up lost in the
poem, like the fallen angels 'endlessly perplexed', yet, you feel,
this huge complexity is not a labyrinth. It may refer to volume
on volume of commentary and doctrinal dispute, but its basic
reference is to a story simple and short, however enigmatic in
what it leaves out.

This disparity, the sense of central simplicity in outward in-
volutions, may emerge as at the core of one's reactions to the
poem when one has read it wholly. It can be approached in
many ways—by a study of literary forms (yet there is no real
parallel in epic), by a study of Milton's thought and reading
particularly as revealed by his prose works (yet the bearing of
these on the poems is obscure both in theory and practice), by
consideration of the development of the doctrines related to the
origin of sin, which will reveal the continued importance of the
story (yet again this will take us far from the world of the poem),
or by assembling a history of attitudes to poetry and its function
and attempting to form an idea of Milton's likely attitude to his
art, of our own distinctive attitudes to literature, and of how

their differences may distort, or at least influence, our reading. Each of these approaches yields something of value and heightens our understanding and appreciation. Yet each has drawbacks, which stem principally from a tendency to isolate the hypothetical intention of the poet, a prose content extracted from the poem, or to see the poem as a sort of complicated aesthetic castle, with skilful brickwork and a certain amount of intriguing stucco. It may be that an approach through conceptions of myth takes in much of these other approaches—warts and all—but I think it does have the merit of not isolating art and content while allowing us to consider each without elaborate intellectual contortions.

Defining 'myth', or, as it may be felt, asserting a convenient selection of definitions for a practical purpose, is no easy task. It is obvious that when we talk of the myth of Prometheus we are thinking of something different from, for example, a dramatic poem or even the content of a dramatic poem by Aeschylus or Shelley. And so it is also with the rebellion of Satan or the Fall of Adam and Eve. Myth in general usage is not a particular story and its expression, but some sort of story-pattern. Very possibly the events of the story, at least as portrayed in the versions we have, never occurred. What did occur was the repeated impulse to retell this story, and it is more with the development of the common impulse than with the distinctions between the various versions of the story that I am concerned in my selection of poems and a novel.

The common impulse of a sense of the transience of beauty begets elegies, sonnets, romances and lyrical works in many forms, and the distinctive events of story attached to each example clearly differ very widely. The same is true of the sense of evil and the search for an origin which may seem in a modest way to make sense of it. It will beget a tale orally recited innumerable times and fragmentarily recorded, or a complex epic, a cycle of plays, a novel, even a lyrical poem. The form will depend on the preference and abilities of the artist and the beliefs and preferences of his age. Clearly, the number of literary works which are produced from impulses analogous to those which, in this case, inspired the biblical myth, is vast, and many which do not employ the biblical story can be found when that story is still largely employed.

Nonetheless, it does seem to me that there is a broad development away from the biblical story and the conceptions of myth and of literature which are associated with the use of it. This process seems to me to throw some light on *Paradise Lost*, and I consider it and *Paradise Lost* in the first section of this book. The second and third sections look at the ways to and from Milton's poem. But, while *Paradise Lost* may occupy a crucial position, it is not in itself the main subject of this book. That is rather changing attitudes to myth, to literature, and therefore to life, as they appear in these versions of the Fall.

PART I

Where Two Ways Meet

1. A Survey

'There runs through modern criticism the fantasy of a
second Fall of Man . . . The Second Fall seems to result
from the introduction of scientific utilitarian values and
modes of thought into the world of choice between good
and evil . . .'

Stephen Spender

If you are considering the Fall story in English literature, the
first version which occurs to you will almost certainly be *Paradise
Lost*. Despite its obscurities or perversities (depending on your
view) it remains the grandest design, the most impressive imaginative construction of certain events which, whether or not they
happened, for many people could or should have happened, or
in some ways are always happening.

Yet *Paradise Lost* has often been held to be deeply flawed. On
this I do not propose to tilt with critical windmills, but merely to
state a position. In my view, what we may call the universality
of *Paradise Lost* stems less from a clash between Milton's beliefs
and the gist of his sources or his interpretation of them, than
from an ambiguity in his approach to his dedicated task—less
from a clash between the argumentative, dogmatic side of his
nature and the emotional and imaginative side, than from an
artistic duality which his historical position in the development
of literary attitudes to a considerable extent imposed on him,
thereby reinforcing those individual factors.

But of course these basic clashes in Milton's mind, the determination with which Puritan Milton, with a brain steeped in all
the available doctrine and dogma, yet steeped his imagination
in the aspirations, the colour, the glorification of the physical
world and heroic achievement to which he responded in Renaissance literature, are most certainly not to be discounted. When

7

we compare Milton with Gerard Manley Hopkins, a poet on a much smaller scale, and religiously of different persuasions, we note that whilst both are artificers loading every rift with ore, conscious at every moment of the manifold effects of every word in its particular position, Hopkins, wrestling with partly similar conflicts, violently forges his short poems from the very stuff of the conflict, whereas Milton, by contrast, achieves a mingling, if precariously, of the warring elements and produces a work of epic stature. It seems to me beyond doubt that the greatness of *Paradise Lost* as well as our uneasiness with it stems from these divisions of impulse, from what are largely contrasted modes of thought, and even contrasted world views, as well as from the intrusion and argument of idiosyncratic and personal doctrines in a myth which makes its appeal to layers in our minds which are deeper than those concerned with argument and justification.

Having said this, however, I do not wish to urge this point so much as to dwell on the artistic question which in part goes parallel to it. In this book I consider *Paradise Lost* first because I see it as a crux, a turning point in poetic attitudes, embodying what had happened and what was to happen. In *Paradise Lost* there meet two views of myth and two conceptions of poetry. I consider the first of these in the Old English *Genesis* and the first Book of *The Faerie Queene*, and the second in a brief review of Romantic attitudes and in Golding's *Lord of the Flies*. This is not to suggest that in general *Paradise Lost* represents some sort of deadline, that before it you wrote poetry one way and after it you wrote poetry (or prose) another way. Clearly attitudes of this sort do not evolve with such nice simplicity. There is rather a continued process of slow change in which *Paradise Lost*, when we take the Fall myth as an example, occupies a critical position, to which our attention is drawn as much by its magnitude as by its suitability for analysis in this regard. No doubt some unread and perhaps unwritten work (which would however be of approximately similar date) might well be a better example; but the argument is wasted if it throws no light on works worth reading and therefore one may as well minimise the theory and consider the works themselves.

Broadly, the two conceptions are of the 'developed story' and the 'personal myth'. In the one, you take as a firm base what happened, what is generally believed to have happened, or what is written. This you develop and expand by the process of 'invention'. You fill in the details. To bald sketches you give flesh and blood. This will of course reduce generality, but you hope that the myth has a strong enough shape to show through the development. Essentially, your attitude is retrospective; what happened or was written is of unique importance either because, paradoxically, it is specially rounded and typical—as the sea-shore pebble preserves the ideal character of pebbles in general yet is itself an individual pebble—or because the events are presumed to have exercised some influence, are still 'significant'. This 'significance' is a balancing item to the retrospective; you may look back to the authority, but your moral concern is with the present and what may come of it. You may by research or imagination arrive at some notion of how it 'really' was, or you may—and in so doing you will rub shoulders with the alternative conception—endeavour to bring it all up to date. But finally, for whatever reason, you are retelling a story.

The alternative conception does not start from this objective basis, and its concern is more patently with the present and future. From personal experience there emerges a story which, in varying degree, comes to bear a close but primarily thematic relationship with the established source. Only as it unfolds will it begin to appear that the work deeply parallels the traditional form, that, perhaps unconsciously, it springs from the same needs and impulses. The place of 'bringing up to date' varies very much in this according to the particular instance. I suspect that the Old English poet's version of the *Genesis* story was brought up to date for more than one reason—perhaps to make it apparently 'significant', perhaps because to a considerable degree he or his sources thought in heroic terms when literature (or recitation) was concerned, and could frame no other conception of society, perhaps because circumstances imposed a press-

ing need for realism in ideals which would not be met by a
pastoral idyll. On the other hand, the thing may be brought up
to date in a more everyday manner—Golding's works provide
more than one instance of this, whilst in general they illustrate
personal myth as well as the bringing up to date of the authority. By a process analogous to class-consciousness and adjustment to it, one may in literature adjust style. I think there is
something of this in the Miltonic grand style; it is not merely
grand in itself but designed to give an appropriate grandeur to
a story which in biblical form, however inspired, is abbreviated
and simplified; our first parents must have been highly intel-
ligent beings, not bumpkins in breeches (or fig leaves), and the
style and discourse should answer to the fact.

If I say that the urge to modernise rubs shoulders with the
personal myth, it is clear that other shoulders rub as well. These
notions of developed story and personal myth are not pigeon-
holes into which various works may be dropped leaving nothing
hanging over the edges, but points of view from which we may
survey as they go to and fro, various works and various aspects
of the same work. Nonetheless, I think that in the development
of English literature a shift of emphasis does take place from one
to the other and that *Paradise Lost* derives much of its scope from
being situated at the cross-roads.

Terms such as 'the poet's mind' or 'conscious' and 'unconscious'—which I use only when I can see no short alternative—are to be understood as terms of convenience. I have no
knowledge that the arguments of Adam and Eve, to be resolved
by the categorical assertion of obedience to Adam as he is to be
obedient to God, bear any relation to squabbles of Mr and Mrs
Milton and I doubt if *Paradise Lost* would be improved for me
if I had such information. I suppose that Piggy and Jack and the
others draw in a somewhat specialised and, it may be, exaggerated manner upon boys whom Mr Golding has observed. It is
hard to believe that they do not. But our interest will depend on
whether we ourselves have met their like as well and can
conceive from mainly obscure recollections a composite being

who resembles Jack or Piggy. Equally, we cannot know how large loomed the biblical *Genesis* in the mind of Spenser, or of Wordsworth or Coleridge, when they formed and wrote their own versions. One cannot even satisfactorily define the moment of forming or writing when the work may be said first to be in its finished form. What will be of interest will be the variety and nature of the apparent parallels to that story in the works as we have them. And, supposing that it could be established of the personal element that the characters did bear some intricate relationship to persons of the artists' acquaintance (and it would have to be intricate), to know, and knowing to quantify, the conscious intention in that relationship would certainly be impossible. Therefore, I leave it as an open question whether Milton was aware of the duality of his epic and whether the works in the third part of this book were *intended* to contribute to or to rehearse the Fall myth. That they do so, however, seems to me clear.

*   *   *

I have referred to the 'Fall myth' and outlined two attitudes to myth and artistic conceptions which go with them, but the nature of myth is debatable, and the development of the debate goes hand in hand with the changing attitude to art, to the very function and nature of a poem or a novel. So it is necessary to consider myth, and the Fall myth in particular, to arrive at working definitions.

The story of a Fall of Man, of a Fall of Angels, of a Fall of a God, is common to civilisations throughout the ages. Its persistence is evidence that it contains, whether or not it answers, certain perennial concerns of man. The fallen state is the human state as we know it. The unfallen state is the eternal might-have-been. Whether heroically the human state is preferred to the dreams of what might have been, or whether lamentably imperfection is deeply realised, the central concerns remain the same.

From the eighteenth century onwards we may take it that 'myth', in popular usage, is opposed to truth or reality. It takes on much of the work which the word 'fable' did for earlier ages.[1] But, as popular usage distinguishes myth from reality, so critical and philosophical discussions come increasingly to view myth as a precious embodiment of an insight into primal problems and even as a revelation of prime truths. So far from being opposed to actual reality, it represents a refined perception of true reality, albeit only available to a more sophisticated and limited public.

A poetic myth is an inherited pattern of thought, the skeleton plot, whose participants are in a significant way typified. If they are of the world of the gods they are eternal forces among whom struggles may take place with grave consequences for the humbler beings below (if they have yet been created); if they are from the dull sublunary world they are embodiments of certain types in whom, more often than not, some particular urge (such as that to exceptional knowledge and power) is predominant. A myth may represent the relation of these two classes of being and thereby convey an insight into the middle state of man. Such a myth is not formed by an individual, whether or not in the past some hypothetical being created the seeds for it from his fears and his ambitions, but in the unconscious of a civilisation seeking to adjust its fears to aspirations partly archetypal and inherited, partly new and peculiar to a period of time, or to an individual's own predicament. It is built upon by a process perhaps not largely conscious, and only from time to time is the pressure such that it is momently forced upwards into consciousness, expressed in a miracle of rare device, to sum up the feelings and thoughts of an era.[2]

It is not easy to determine the views of earlier ages on this matter. We may assume that the *Genesis* story was believed in a fundamentalist way, but the edges of such a belief are very hard to define. When medieval writers list types of interpretation—such as literal, typological, or anagogical—we are apt to wonder whether meanings can be codified in such ways and whether the supposition that they could was ever more than academic. And, wondering this, we go on to speculate whether their beliefs were so very far from our own after all. I think, however, that it is probable that the fundamental and literal belief, the belief that two persons called Adam and Eve at some remote time existed, just as they are said to exist in *Genesis*, occupied a larger part of people's minds than it now does, and that what to many of us is the primary belief—that the story is in some way a symbol for a possible interpretation of our own state which has not basically varied from that day to this—was on the whole less prominent but was still present. Certainly it was held that the situation of Adam was in some way repeated in the life of each person after him, but equally certainly it was held, in hotly disputed ways, that each person after him was influenced by the prior behaviour of Adam. The conception that the final form of the myth is always ahead, that the thing is dynamic and evolutionary and we are all the time adding to it as we rehearse it, is a modern one.

One has to guard against the idea, where literature is concerned, that because in a certain work we are confronted with a revered and important myth that work is, as a result, necessarily important and to be revered. In an effort to combat this convenient assumption I take as a starting point two statements of C. S. Lewis, where a myth is held to be 'a particular kind of story which has value in itself, a value independent of its embodiment in any literary work . . . whose pleasure depends hardly at all on usual narrative attractions such as suspense and surprise'. 'The value of myth is not a specifically literary value, nor the appreciation of myth a specifically literary appreciation.'[3]

It seems to me clear that Lewis did not mean to imply in this that once we have isolated the 'myth' we shall be left with the 'literature'. No doubt it is possible to retell the Fall myth in a form devoid of literary merit—Dryden, for one, came near to doing so in *The State of Innocence*. I think that Lewis believed— as would Spenser and Milton whose work he discussed—that the greatness of *Paradise Lost* cannot be divorced from the mythical stature of its subject matter, even if we concede that by 'subject matter' here is meant rather more than is meant by Lewis's stark definition of myth.

If they are inseparable in this way, changing ways of viewing myth and of viewing literature will go together, and it seems to me broadly true that they do so. There is a change from the use of an accepted myth, related to a background of accepted and generally agreed beliefs and values which the writer can employ with some assurance of being understood (even as he will re-interpret them as he writes), to the situation where the writer creates, indeed grows, his own myth, although aware of the accepted versions and paralleling and commenting on them.

This change, so far as the Fall myth is concerned, emerges from an ever-increasing stress on the typicality, the repetitive conception of the Fall, and a decreasing stress on its presumed historical nature. If it was not the stealing of the apple which precipitated us into a vale of tears, then conceivably it was a baleful streak in our genetic make-up, or a traumatic experi-ence which, revealed to us as is the eating of an apple, may lead us, if not to serenity, at least to self-knowledge and acceptance. It is true that neither of these influences appears voluntary to quite the same degree as does the eating of the apple; but then how voluntary that was has always been open to question. Again, there is a possible distinction between the Fall as a catastrophic event central to revealed religion and the Fall as a typical moment of sin; yet the two are related and have been related from the earliest times. On the first view the story of Adam and Eve, or of the Angels (which pushes it back a stage), represents an event or a hypothesised event which governs all subsequent human life. On the other view, the entry of evil into the mind of a child, or the evil at a critical moment in the mind of an adult, is a repetition neither more nor less significant than the first time it may once have occurred. Once this view has emerged, we may see versions of the Fall as versions not simply of the Adam and Eve story, but as versions of a myth of which the Adam and Eve story is itself a version rather than the progenitor.

Pope's *Essay on Man* shows the trend. 'For Pope's age and Pope as poet (whatever may have been the case for Pope as man) even this story (of the Fall) had lost, perhaps, its full imaginative availability.' Professor Mack's suggestive reading[4] of the poem is by analogy with *Paradise Lost* (where, however, a number of distinctively personal elements have already entered the myth). The Garden of Eden is represented by the world at large with its manifold temptations, and the paradise lost and to be regained is not, as it is for Milton, partly a state of mind and partly a celestial life to come, but rather wholly inward, the fully known self, ordered and controlled—a theme which Milton himself, in *Paradise Regained*, would consider 'above heroic'. Here, then, is a poem which presents none of the apparatus of the *Genesis* story, but which is, in its own abstract and inwardly-directed way, yet a version of the Fall, and a version which takes further the 'repetitive' element. Its object is decidedly not to retell the story. The poem is, rather, self-contained, a version arising out of impulses parallel to those behind the biblical version.

It may seem a far cry from this intellectual conception to the world of the Romantics. But, if we substitute for Pope's Chain of Being the less analytical conception of a universe where a vision, comprehensive if sadly fugitive, can embrace 'the meanest flower that blows' and 'the unfettered clouds and region of the heavens', recognising all as the 'types and symbols of eternity', and if we substitute for the perfectible individual of Pope's poem the solitary visionary Wordsworth or the solitary unrecognisable mariner with 'strange power of speech' in Coleridge's poem— if we make these and other comparisons we are driven to the conclusion that the move towards the study of the state of mind, the internalisation of battles which might once have been rendered as between knight and dragon, God and Satan, is a further continuing process.

The differences, however, are equally clear. Wordsworth's visionary gleam is dependent on a solitude which is both transitory and not unmixed with a sense of guilt. It is a bliss from which he falls and his fall he intimates, with varying conviction, to be something of a *felix culpa*, a fortunate fall, in which he finds at least the hope that the love of nature leads on to the love of man. For Coleridge also the fall is a mixed affair, the gaining of vision whereby the gifted are outcast, or conversely a desperate lack of vision is the fallen state. For both Wordsworth and Coleridge these ideas followed on an investigation of the limits of free will. They speculated on the extent to which 'free' or 'not free' could adequately define the complex state of a mind contemplating action, particularly unnatural action, and therefore on the justice of the retribution which Nature delivered for her violation. Particularly were they driven to contemplate the child, who was, it seemed, beatifically incapable of such perversion or, at the least, as in Wordsworth's *Nutting*, capable of education by the 'low breathings' of the Nature he had offended. Their problem was to substitute an adult and conscious way of life consonant with the intuitive virtues and vision which they ascribed to the child. It was against later and less potent forms of the innocent child cult that Golding in *Lord of the Flies* reacted.

Keats's conception, whilst also contrasting two stages of life, was somewhat different. There are the mature and the immature visions. He tries to find vindication that he is not but a 'dreaming thing', but will move on, with the poetic dedication of Milton and Wordsworth, to sing of 'the agonies, the strife of human hearts'. But this symbol of a poet of new human concern, this Apollo, makes no direct appearance in *Hyperion*, and the belief that 'on our heels a fresh perfection treads', to supersede the fallen Titans, the outmoded visionaries, finds no fulfilment in the poem. Yet it may be said to be realised, in a tentative and imperfect manner, by the very writing of the second version of *Hyperion*, by the replacing of the symbol by the poet himself.

From this survey of developments after Milton we may draw certain conclusions. The Romantic and the post-Romantic versions of the Fall are concerned less with Adam and Eve than with the role and character of the artist in a society whose values are felt by the sensitives to be unstable. The artist is privileged to a special vision of the unfallen state, but this privilege is itself a curse and he the more fallen for possessing it. Fresh impulse is given to the treatment of the myth as of a recurrent event. Whether it is at birth or at the coming of adolescence, the individual falls, or else he does so by some decisive act the precise moment of whose initiation and whose motivation remain impenetrably mysterious.

Though the sense of guilt, or 'remorse', may be especially burdensome in these versions, the extent of responsibility remains more blurred, and the investigation of the problems posed by the idea of free will seems to become of less intense interest during the century than the bleak contrast of what is with what might have been. Commonly the Fall is not re-enacted before our eyes but reconstructed by its participants in later life. The predominant attitude is retrospective and introverted—the regard is not to the authority of a previous version but to a previous stage of the speaker's life. Wordsworth, like the Ancient Mariner, is under compulsion to recall and live again the earlier experiences 'felt along the blood' in order to write a poem, to establish his predicament here and now. Cain, the direct heir to the Fall, an outcast with a sense of living within unreasonable limitations to his freedom, is of more absorbing interest than are Adam and Eve. For Clough, in his *Mystery of the Fall*, Cain kills Abel and marvels at the facility with which this novelty of death can be accomplished. Alas, he is eventually consumed by guilt welling inexplicably from within him and achieves nothing approaching peace of mind until the 'mighty mythus of the Fall', of which Eve has dreamed, and at which Adam has scoffed, is for the first time mentioned to him by his parents. Whether Adam, or Eve, or Cain—or the poet—in the literal sense 'believes in' the Fall is an issue not resolved by the poem. It is enough that the idea be presented to Cain. And in this respect this profound and original fragment by Clough is typical of the Romantic and post-Romantic versions; the Fall, as theme, is vital and pervasive, but there is no substantial and completed work which recreates the myth of the Fall itself and (as if by connection) the Fall myth is intimately bound up with the effort of the artist to discover both his own nature and his own status.

*   *   *

When Stephen Spender referred to 'the fantasy of a second Fall of Man'[5] running through modern criticism he had in mind a common idea that personal values and accepted faith were at some stage (and the period varies according to the exponent) gradually replaced by impersonal forces, a cold world of science in which worth is decided by expediency and satisfaction is related to utilitarian criteria. An associated fantasy is Eliot's, that 'in the seventeenth century, a dissociation of sensibility set in, from which we have never recovered', language, thought, and feeling became specialised, narrower, more 'refined' but at the risk of being effete.[6] Subsequent poets no longer 'possessed a mechanism of sensibility which could devour any kind of experience'. In a rather different sense, T. E. Hulme employed the myth to distinguish between Classic and Romantic; the Romantic regards human nature as like a well, 'a reservoir full of possibilities', whereas the party 'which regards him as a very finite and fixed creature, I call the classical.' In a word, the Romantic is without a fundamental sense of the Fall.[7]

I do not intend to argue the merits of these views. 'Fantasies' they must be if they are regarded as rules, but as points of view for particular purposes they had and have their uses. What seems to me of interest in them is that the critic venturing into theory stumbles on that same association of the Fall myth with the nature and function of art as we have noted emerging in Romantic versions. Basically it is of the visionary whose medium is literary art, and the vision does not exist without the art, for the art becomes the vision as Keats becomes his Apollo who therefore cannot put in an appearance. As we experience this literature by living it through, as the poet experienced it in some sense by living it through, we cannot separate myth from its expression. If we are unable to appreciate the poet's position, in however pale a measure, have not felt his conflicts, and cannot enter into Keats's sparrow as it picks the gravel outside his window, then we are barred in a way in which we are not barred from poetry composed for a less literate and more restricted public in an earlier age. Therefore, it seems to me that we arrive at the paradox that modern literary art which disengages itself and fully 'embodies', literature which may aspire to the condition of music or of sculpture, is in its effect, for all its integral uncertainties and inextricable morals, curiously dogmatic. In the very claim to freedom, to be judged by purely aesthetic standards (whatever they may be), it imposes on itself serious limitation.

There is a solidity and an objectivity about developed story which we miss in personal myth. For the Old English author of *Genesis*, however complete and realistic of his time his work may be, the truth is regarded as external to it, abstract if to be defined, spiritual if not. The work refers to a body of thought already shaped and rounded, the myth or truth of the Fall, the story of Adam and Eve or the Fall of the Angels. It is not that the Old English poet is unaware that boys have within them the beast or that Golding is unaware that Eve allegedly ate an apple, but that, being confronted with the same sense of disparity between what is or was and what might have been, the one chooses to write about boys and the other about Eve. Again, one may follow the Old English poem as a spectator, but one must join in *Lord of the Flies* as a participant, for the style manipulates the reader. It would be unjust to conclude that the work about Eve is inherently likely to be of stature, and it would also be irrelevant since, if this change in the nature of and attitude to myth has developed, it is not a development from which the writer of today can opt out. The point is rather that what may be called 'representational' art—that which is in the crudest sense the less representational—is, by its consciousness of truth outside it, partly released from the danger of material not shaped into art and a miscellany of styles whose effects may not always precisely achieve their particular objects. The blurring effect of such material seems to me apparent in *Lord of the Flies*. It is not absent from *Paradise Lost*, but Milton's work uniquely bridges the two conceptions of myth.

From a religious point of view the change from developed story to personal myth does not much concern us here. Clearly it can be argued that the changing view of myth goes hand in hand with a process of secularisation, as the changing view of literature and of the role of its creator goes hand in hand with the growth of literacy. I do not propose to argue it here, except to say that what one means by 'secularisation' and 'literacy' is evidently the crux of the matter. It is a question whether the mass ability to read a newspaper works in favour of or militates against the wider appreciation of literature and its enhancement of everyday life, and it is a question whether an individual's myth of the Fall is a dilution of the biblically recorded myth or whether it is of equal validity because formed in a similar way from similar needs. These are not questions within my present scope.

2. *Paradise Lost*

'Were it not for the happy notion that a man's poetry is
not at all affected by his opinions or indeed character and
mind altogether, I fear the *Paradise Lost* would be utterly
unsaleable except for waste paper to the University.'

A. H. Clough

In some respects *Paradise Lost* does not strike one immediately as
mythic. It has not that clearly shaped and easily memorable
outline, perhaps, nor the gaps in the action and omissions or
simplifications of motive, implying insoluble mystery, to which
we often apply the term. It is a poem, it has been said, so
densely argued, so intricately wrought with internal allusions
and multiple accounts of the same words and actions, not to
mention its copious external references mythological and otherwise, that it is liable to beget a sort of neurosis in the reader. It is
full of comment on its own action, whether that issues directly
from its author or from a dramatically conceived narrator.

I would maintain, however, that it is in fact mythic in two
senses. It is so in that it follows the outline and in fact manages to
include most of the detail of the *Genesis* story and embodies those
situations. But, over and above this, it attempts the embodiment
of a personal myth—a myth Puritan and Augustinian in
emphasis—concerning the necessity in all spheres of life of
obedience, which it essays to define in a special sense, and love,
which it relates to obedience. This myth is something of a
rationalisation, an interpretation, of the other, and adds scenes
and arguments to the basic shape of the authority. The two
elements of myth seem to clash, in a way which in one respect
tempers the success of the poem, and in another can be seen as
intensifying the meaning and nature of the Fall.

It was essential for Milton's purposes that the relationship of

21

God and man evince general parallels with the relationship of man and woman; the fall of Eve and Adam had to exemplify a breakdown in both relationships and initiated by the obeying member of the pair. Eve disobeyed Adam (and partly as a consequence disobeyed God), and Adam disobeyed God. Yet God must control all events, so that an argument had to be advanced to allow of free will (on which depends their responsibility). Moreover, as Adam forms part of the one relationship, so does God of the other, and therefore God has to be both detached and involved, as some possible laxness on the part of Adam must and must not precipitate the action of Eve. An uncertainty in this respect of setting things going reads very plausibly on the human level but in Milton's heaven the dual note required of God results in an intermittently impressive but generally highly unsympathetic deity.

The poem marks a turning point in versions of the Fall myth. In its re-creation of the biblical story and its magnificent accretion of detail from the commentaries[1] and the imagination, in its clear purpose of retelling the authority in such a way as to bring it home to the contemporary reader, it is evidently a story highly developed. In the direction which is given to this story, and importantly in the parallels between earthly and heavenly levels which its structure forces on our attention, it is equally clearly an example of personal myth. For it to be an unqualified success these conceptions would have to work to the same end and emerge as a unity. For present purposes I separate them here more than a reader of the poem feels them in practice to be separated. Nonetheless, it seems to me that they do not emerge as an unqualified unity. At more than one crucial moment we are obliged to choose between the implication of the developed story and that of the personal myth and, for myself, I sympathise with the uncertain motives and essential realism on the personal level of the story when the choice arises.

But the personal myth is not merely an argument or a point of dogma. It is rather what we see when we look at the poem from a particular viewpoint. If that argument or dogma con-

cerns a comparison of obedience to God and of obedience to
man, we shall find the myth centred on the human level, because it is there that the definition of obedience is most debatable
and most readily to be attempted and there that the sketchy
events of the story may be filled in and given particular direction
which makes sense when tested 'on the pulses', in Keats's
phrase; in heaven, consistency is more simply an intellectual
matter, though on this too more is to be said.

* * *

Towards the end of *Paradise Lost* 'our Sire', having made a
series of false inferences about the course of history which
Michael reveals to him, and having been judiciously and tact-
fully corrected in these conclusions by Michael, representing,
thus instructed, the height of knowledge which fallen man may
achieve—our Sire voices the dilemma of the *felix culpa*, the
Fortunate Fall, which represents in effect, either an acknowledgement of the supreme mercy of God conveyed through the
sacrifice of his Son and the gift of Grace, or the triumph of the
human point of view during the action of the Fall:

> 'full of doubt I stand
> Whether I should repent me now of sin
> By me done and occasioned, or rejoyce
> Much more, that much more good thereof shall spring,
> To God much glory, more good will to Men
> From God, and over wrath grace shall abound'
> (XII, 473–8).

Michael refrains from comment. To the reader, however, it is a
question which cries for answer from the poem. God suffered the
war in heaven to continue so that the military prowess of his
Son should be fully demonstrated. He placed an unnecessary
guard on Eden in the full knowledge that Satan would find a
way in. The Fall, not simply because its myth decreed it so, but

from the logic of the Divine within the poem, had to occur, the Fall portrayed as the gravest sin, producing suicidal misery in Adam and Eve and a vision of history made tolerable only by the mystical notions of grace and redemption. All this was for the greater glory of God. Was it also for the greater happiness of Man?

That depends very much on how we view the state of innocence in the poem. There are not wanting indications that life in Eden did not strike the Milton who could not praise a fugitive and cloistered virtue as fully satisfying. Those aspects of it which seem nearest to satisfying (most notably the love of Adam and Eve) do not appear peculiar to Paradise as he presents it, but possible to realise in the fallen world. The portrayal of the love, the breach of confidence, the accusations, and the reconciliation, of Adam and Eve, form a major strand in the poem. It is so fully realised by Milton that it rivals in interest the nature of the interference with it. The historical myth is from this view but the occasion of the separation of Adam and Eve which is perfectly plausible on the human level. There are suggestions in the characterisation of Adam and Eve which militate against the idea of total free will which Milton and his advocates within the poem put forward; in a word, the story of obedience between Adam and Eve, the personal myth, was, at the depth in which it is realised by Milton, too continuous and too realistic to fit the historical myth, in its problematic simplicity, as the fruit is eaten. It is by no means clear to what extent Adam and Eve fell or what paradise they lost.

*   *   *

Abdiel, whose view is supported by the narrator on this matter, distinguishes the true Obedience before the angels engage in battle with Satan:

'Unjustly thou depravst it with the name
Of Servitude to serve whom God ordains,

Or Nature; God and Nature bid the same,
When he who rules is worthiest, and excells
Them whom he governs. This is servitude,
To serve th'unwise, him who hath rebelld
Against his worthier, as thine now serve thee,
Thyself not free, but to thyself enthralld'

(VI, 174–81).

Even whilst in heaven, Satan did not, according to Gabriel, 'obey' in the mystical sense, but was subservient for his own reasons:

'who more then thou
Once fawnd, and cringd, and servilly adord
Heaven's awful Monarch? Wherefore but in hope
To dispossess Him and thyself to reigne?'

(IV, 958–61).

The following of whom is 'worthiest' is Obedience, and the serving of 'th'unwise' is Servitude. Obedience is a service which is perfect freedom, whilst Servitude is thralldom. However, Obedience is a state of mind, not a matter of whose flag one has at one's head or to whom one casts the vote. Satan in heaven went through the motions of obedience to 'Heaven's awful Monarch', but since this service was not based on a recognition of the Monarch's supreme qualities and following right to rule, his state was not of obedience but of fawning and cringing. In theory at least, had Satan been more fit to rule than was God, Milton could have approved his rebellion. It is therefore crucial either that our belief in God's goodness is such that we do not for a moment doubt that he is the one to obey, or that he is within the poem shown to be such; in practice Milton relies both on the assumption and on the demonstration, but the demonstration seems not only to fail to produce the desirable notion, but appears in places actually to contradict it. There remains the assumption, the premise, that God even in a rather different conception, a Being who in any case is incomprehensible and can only be suggested in the vaguest way by literary portraiture, is supremely worthy of obedience. But this assumption, on which at least for the modern reader the poem rests, has to fight with the deeply human portrayal of Adam and Eve for our sympathies.

Obedience and Servility, Freedom and Licence, Reason and Passion or Fancy—these are the oppositions among which the action moves. For Milton, as for Michael, they are all interconnected:

> 'Since thy original lapse, true Libertie
> Is lost, which alwayes with right Reason dwells
> Twinnd, and from her hath no dividual being;
> Reason in man obscur'd, or not obey'd
> Immediatly inordinate desires
> And upstart Passions catch the Government
> From Reason, and to servitude reduce
> Man till then free'
>
> (XII, 83–90).

Obedience to the right leader is the key to Milton's psychology as well as to his theocracy, and the right leader is Reason. Since the Fall, Reason is obscured and, so Milton goes on to say, not only is Reason not obeyed by the other faculties in the individual, but Reason no longer provides an unerring guide to the choice of the right ruler outside the individual in society. Man, who was formerly obedient truly and therefore free, becomes disobedient and enthralled to himself and to whatever base authority may seek to exploit him. This follows both as a result of the fact that Reason is no longer able to detect what is right, and because God 'subjects him from without to violent lords', apparently as a retribution or warning. In such a way Milton saw the Restoration, a case where, since Man was fallen, his Reason misled him and his passions triumphed, to impose a tyranny and thralldom, paralleled by a divinely imposed retribution of 'Justice, and some fatal curse annexed' (98–9).

It is above all, on the purely human level, in love that the issue of obedience becomes crucial. The distinction between obedience which is thralldom and obedience which is liberty, rests in the attitude of the obeyer and obeyed, and this attitude is a voluntary matter entirely. 'Our voluntary service he requires, Not our necessitated', Raphael explains (V, 528–30). Obedience which can be broken, if occasion merits, or maintained despite the severest 'test'—a word repeatedly used and responsible for some of our misgivings about God—is alone obedience as distinct from compulsion. This obedience is of the nature of love and loyalty, not the carrying out of a set of rules —it is an attitude. 'Freely we serve, Because we freely love' (V, 538–9).

In Milton's view of Adam and Eve, and their relationship, we observe some difficulty with this theory. It was Milton's settled belief that man was made nearer the image of God than was Eve, and was imbued with superior rational powers. It was, then, natural that he should feel that it was woman's role to obey her husband, though he accepted that there might be individual exceptions, and grounds for them, to this arrangement, which was a matter of the obedience of the less wise to the more wise. The difficulty arises from the fact that this was for Milton so important that he made it typical of the state of man both before and after the Fall. The biblical account gives some ground for believing that it was a consequence of the Fall ('thy desire shall be to thy husband, and he shall rule over thee'— *Gen.* III, 16) and leaves the relations of Adam and Eve in this respect obscure before the Fall. Milton of course does not ignore the change and duly includes it in God's sentence over the woman:

> 'and to thy Husband's will
> Thine shall submit, hee over thee shall rule'
>
> (X, 195–6).

The difficulty of this is analogous to that of the labour to which
man is condemned; in what respect is the situation after the Fall
inferior to that which existed in Paradise?[2] Adam and Eve were
to tend the garden in Paradise and the fact, as is well known,
results in some awkwardness on Milton's part as to how hopeless
a labour and how compulsory a one this was likely to be. Man,
it is true, will in future be dependent on the work to secure his
daily bread (X, 205), but there is more than a hint of truth in
Adam's remark to Eve that

> 'with labour I must earne
> My bread; what harm? Idlenesse had been worse;
> My labour will sustain me . . .'
>
> (X, 1054–6).

As with the disobedience, so with the gardening; the Fall does
not in the event, when we compare the situations before and
after, appear so grave as the poem is at pains to make it seem.

That we are meant to sense a change is, however, beyond
dispute. I take it that the change in the case of obedience in love
is meant to parallel that which he alleges to occur in the case of
obedience in politics; after the Fall, tyranny is possible and an
obedience which is not a service of perfect freedom. What is
questionable is whether this distinction emerges or could
emerge clearly when the one crucial question of obedience on
which the whole action depends (namely, whether or not Adam
and Eve should have gone their separate ways) is settled by
Adam in a manner which, while wholly mature and estimable,
does not strike us as either distinctly pre-lapsarian or impossible
for a post-lapsarian couple to imitate; and yet he is upbraided
for his flexibility with Eve at this juncture.

Consider the relations of Adam and Eve at this critical
moment in the action. Whilst in Eve's view and in that of the
narrator 'much their work outgrew The hands dispatch of two
gardning so wide' (IX, 201–2), in Adam's view the Lord had not
so strictly enjoined this labour as to debar them from refreshment

whether of body or spirit (235–41). This may well be so, but it
is no answer to Eve's fear that there is too much garden for them
to cope with together, which is the reason—so far as we know a
perfectly acceptable one—why Eve suggests separating from
Adam. For 'casual discourse' may bring the day's work to little
if they continue to work side by side. There is of course considerable doubt in the poem how pressing a duty it is for art to
triumph over 'wanton' (IX, 211) nature in Paradise; obviously
if it is too much like hard work the working for their living to
which God is going to sentence them will be no relative hardship, but the mere fact that the work is to an indeterminable
extent unnecessary is not in itself any reason to disbelieve Eve's
argument that they ought to find a more effective way of doing
it. And Adam is reasonable; he values her 'sweet intercourse'
and 'smiles (which) from Reason flow' (they were of course why
he asked God to let him have a companion), but he accepts that
'much converse' may be wearisome and that 'solitude sometimes
is best societie'. He could bear 'short absence', but he is per-
turbed by the danger of the malicious foe of whom they have
been warned and who may tempt them to disobedience or (and
this is his invention, not part of the warning he was given)
'disturb Conjugal love'. From him, Adam, she was made and he
still protects her;

> 'The wife, where danger or dishonour lurks,
> Safest and seemliest by her husband staies,
> Who guards her, or with her the worst endures'
> (IX, 267–9).

Eve is mildly injured by this. Her reaction, one would think,
is that of fallen woman; yet we are not to think so, for it is the
premise of the poem that Eve and Adam do not fall until the
eating of the apple. Before, they are merely 'free to fall', with no
sin in them, and nothing in the character of either can be held
to have predisposed them to fall. In her reply, in which she is
hurt that he 'my firmnesse therefore doubt', she behaves, there-

fore, 'as one who loves, and some unkindnesse meets' (271). We are tempted to say—'well, that's what she *is*'. But the narrator does not say so—she is merely *as* or *like* a lover in receipt of unkindness or distrust. The distinction is, I submit, as awkward as it is necessary. Our first parents meet the constant difficulty within the poem that, if this amount of detail is to be given to their motives and behaviour, it must be humanly credible, but for it to be humanly credible it must smack of ordinary human beings whom we know, and who are in the fallen state. Milton has to maintain that that which has all the appearance of being identity is in fact merely simile.

Adam says that he does not mistrust her. He appeals to love—admitting his own weakness as Eve does not—as the strength which would be lacking if they were separated, the spiritually invigorating love which for him is inseparable from the physical—

> 'I from the influence of thy looks receave
> Access in every Vertue, in thy sight
> More wise, more watchful, stronger . . .'
>
> (309–11).

Eve replies with confidence in her own faith and strength, stating that there is no reason why their enjoyment of Eden should be limited and restricted by the presence of the Foe, and iterating (an opinion which Milton elsewhere emphatically supports)

> 'And what is Faith, Love, Vertue unassaid
> Alone, without exterior help sustain?'

To her Adam repeats the gist of what he has learned from Raphael:

> 'But God left free the Will, for what obeyes
> Reason is free, and Reason he made right.'

He is better endowed with Reason than is she, but in any case, Reason can be 'surpris'd' and 'misinform the Will' of the best of us. He does not abandon his point of view that this is less likely to happen if she is accompanied by him, and enjoins her in plain terms,

> 'Wouldst thou approve thy constancie, approve
> First thy obedience'
>
> (367–8).

Then he permits her to go, touching the heart of the paradox of the true obedience:

> 'Go; for thy stay, not free, absents thee more;
> Go in thy native innocence, relie
> On what thou hast of vertue, summon all,
> For God toward thee hath done his part, do thine'
>
> (373–6).

Thus, letting Eve go, he cryptically repeats Raphael's words to him when he, Adam, fears Eve's love is depriving him of his clear judgement—'Accuse not Nature, shee hath don her part; Do thou but thine' (VIII, 561–2)—which suggests that he believes he is sufficiently asserting himself now (or may be seen as dramatic irony).

To this difference of opinion Adam and Eve will return in their mutual accusations after the Fall. Eve declares,

> 'Too facil then thou didst not much gainsay,
> Nay, didst permit, approve, and fair dismiss.
> Hadst thou been firm and fixt in thy dissent,
> Neither had I transgresst, nor thou with me'
>
> (IX, 1158–61).

Eve is of course humanly evading responsibility by finding an external object to herself to blame. It is idle to speculate whether, had he been firmer, she would have 'transgresst' all the same. Adam replies that he did all he could, since

> 'beyond this had bin force,
> And force upon free Will hath here no place'
>
> (1173–4).

Again, it is idle to speculate how much dissuasion amounts to 'force' and a denial of free will.

This is, in a sense, the crucial scene in the account of the human Fall, and the difficulties it creates are the result of Milton's personal myth concerning obedience as it affects man and woman and as that parallels obedience among the members of a society or to God. I do not think for a moment that we are intended to feel that Adam should have insisted on Eve's remaining with him. Nor do I think that his not doing so represents a weak submission to female wiles. But, as we shall see, Milton has ensured that the latter interpretation cannot be entirely ruled out and, by repeating the phrase 'do thy part', has underlined the critical nature of Adam's decision—he has asserted himself, done his part in this regard as Raphael advised, but not to such an extent as to violate Eve's free will. Should he have done more? Again, he gives no unequivocal order; in that sense Eve does not disobey him. But, plainly, there is no doubt that he wishes her to remain with him, and in that sense she disobeys him. Yet again, it is not *merely* a disobedience of the spirit, because we cannot be entirely sure that the spirit is right.

Evidently this situation is not the same as the outright and 'unreasonable' ban on eating the fruit; although the motive of hubris is not excluded, and creates a problem which cannot be discounted, the general effect of the ban on the fruit by God is that it was arbitrary, and that Milton meant it to be so—it was the pure 'test' of obedience. Adam's wish that Eve stay with him is not of this nature. Much of it may be put down to his perhaps excessive fear of 'danger or dishonour', and his worry that conjugal love is under threat, and much of it is arguable, as Eve argues it. He has also the air of playing a part—he is indeed at this moment the pawn of history and the poem's mechanics. But neither for Adam nor for Eve nor for the reader can this be said to be an arbitrary test of obedience, and moreover the man who gives the orders or states the wish is as much under scrutiny as the person who obeys or disobeys, and this, within the poem, is not the position when God gives commands. It is a scene conditioned by the historical story—it must issue in disaster. Wise after the event, we look back and scrutinise it. We also magnify it; essentially it is a humdrum affair requiring a practical decision of the moment and Eve is not rendered any the less in her 'native innocence' by accepting the offer of free choice. But we are conditioned by knowledge of the myth, and Milton has ensured by echoes and parallels that we see in the scene more than in a moment of fallen reality it could contain.

So, despite the qualifications, the reader stumbles at this place. The disobedience of the spirit seems not totally different from the disobedience of the letter. For Adam, Eve's assertion of free will is indeed a new factor, a shadow on the scene of the wife willingly submissive and admitting her husband's superiority in all things. For us, it is a shadow, not of imperfection but of complication—either a sudden enlargement in the concept of ideal and paradisaical obedience, by which the exercise of free will is not itself an act of disobedience morally reprehensible, or an inadvertent admission of human reality into the perfect enamel of the husband-wife relationship as depicted hitherto in the poem (an admission of it by the fallen author but not with the recognition that it is itself fallen behaviour).

My feeling is that we here tend to see Eve deviating from the moral scheme hitherto depicted and we regard that deviation as sympathetic and even praiseworthy. Adam we would respect less if he stuck doggedly to his insubstantial arguments. One is free to disobey; but, if that disobedience infallibly results in catastrophe, is it any more than a theoretical concept, and is it the case that disobedience infallibly results in catastrophe? The poem does not say so, but that is the effect of its examples. To complete the pattern what we require, but cannot have, is an instance to the contrary or of disobedience to one not asserted to be naturally superior in reason and all other qualities. We have suddenly been thrown into a situation, a human action, where the characters live as disagreeing individuals and yet in the context of a pattern which we cannot assent to as true to experience. To us the action of Adam and Eve here is the action of fallen persons we know and it fits the moral scheme only because of a trick in the data by which men are premised superior to women.

*   *   *

This scene is part of the complex depiction of married love in the poem. Despite the severity of Divine disapproval for Adam's submission to Eve when he eats the apple, the poem is not stinting in its praise of marital love, nor is it unambiguous. A key passage here is the narrator's praise, 'Haile wedded love' in Book IV, where we first see Adam and Eve in Eden (750ff). Milton has written some lines which he apparently deems surprising or remarkable for the situation:

> 'Strait side by side were laid, nor turnd I ween
> Adam from his fair Spouse, nor Eve the Rites
> Mysterious of connubial love refus'd'
>
> (741–3).

The situation is not in fact surprising, although Milton has so stressed the lack of clothes (those 'troublesome disguises') in his efforts to gain wonder that it seems more surprising than it is. The effect of his praise here is to force a quite unnecessary emphasis on the whole scene. This, we are to suppose, is love perfect as it has never been since. It is, he says, 'hypocrites' who form a conception of 'purity and place and innocence' which excludes the rites mysterious, and it is Satan 'who bids abstain' from increase. The intention seems to be to reverse Platonic aspersions on physical love and to regard it both as legitimate pleasure in itself and a necessary furthering of the right to 'increase'. True love is 'founded in Reason, loyal, just, and pure', and has driven 'adulterous lust' off to 'bestial herds'. In fact, so far from being an evil indulgence, this 'perpetual fountain of domestic sweets' befits 'holiest place' and is to be contrasted with

> 'the bought smile
> Of harlots, loveless, joyless, unindeard,
> Casual fruition, nor in Court Amours,
> Mixt Dance, or wanton Mask, or Midnight Ball'
>
> (765–7).

There can be no doubt of Milton's anxiety to portray married love, as it is shown here, as a supremely innocent happiness, a refinement and an essence of the best of love in a fallen world, not different in nature or kind.[3]

Yet in the description of Adam and Eve all is not well. It can of course be argued that the reader first observes the scene as a 'peeping Tom', in a bedroom to which he would not normally have access, and then is disconcerted to discover Satan in the same role, and unfavourably cast in that role. To Satan, the love of our first parents is an object of intense jealousy, contrasted with the sensual 'fierce desire' which does duty in hell (509). It will be natural for him to overdo its sensuous attractions, and if we are embarrassed at the scene and Satan is also embarrassed it follows that our fallen judgement is at fault.[4]

But I do not think that this will do. It is not simply that we, fallen beings, approach the setting with fallen feelings, and, finding them in graver form in the Foe, realise by a sort of shock reaction that we too are wrong. It is more that Milton is self-conscious in his use of this material and overdoes things. Eve responds to Adam's first speech (411–439) (which is itself full of awkward factual exposition) with the first example of her 'true' unfallen vein of just submission. She praises him as her 'Guide and Head' and claims that his lot is harder than hers since, being inferior, she is not really true 'like consort' for Adam. Indeed, Adam, like God, can have no true like consort—the hierarchical scheme of things means that he is even with her bound to be alone. There is no criticism of her implicit in this; it is merely a fact that both are

> 'Not equal, as their sex not equal seemd;
> For contemplation hee and valour formed,
> For softness shee and sweet attractive grace,
> Hee for God onely, shee for God in him'
>
> (296–9).

'God is thy law, thou mine', Eve puts it. Her seductive submissiveness is as she was created. But the description of Eve seems to suggest rather more than merely such an order. We can accept the state of her hair 'disshevel'd' and in wanton ('careless' —but there is a pun, and the untended plants in the garden are also 'wanton') ringlets; this we might say is the hairdo of nature not subjected to art. But when her appearance implies 'subjection, but requir'd with gentle sway' the hasty qualification makes us uneasy, and there is about her yielding with 'sweet reluctant amorous delay' and 'coy submission' something over-suggestive.

We cannot in any simple way read into these suggestions the idea that here is the potential source of man's undoing, for that undoing is dependent solely on free will. On the other hand, if this appearance is typical of the fallen world it is the more remarkable to find it in Eden. What occurs is, I suspect, accidental; a mildly distorted view of the fallen world is projected on to the image of the unfallen Eve. We can say that here is love without shame, seduction without evil, that it is the fallen state of man which can only recognise good against evil rather than pure good. But this will hardly account for the effects of the description where there seems to be suggestion over and above that which is functionally required. No doubt the absence of a suitable language is partly to blame. 'Coy submission' and 'myster-

ious parts' give an impression of linguistic titillation which is
only made more forcible by the announcement that follows, even
if 'mysterious' is taken strictly in its celebratory sense:

> 'Then was not guiltie shame, dishonest shame
> Of Nature's works, honor dishonorable . . .'

The 'dishonest shame' emerges unhappily in the very obliquity
of the language, its peculiar mode of suggestion and generalisation, its abstract nouns, its negatives, its 'sweet reluctance'
even as it makes a claim for frankness:

> 'Nor gentle purpose, nor endearing smiles
> Wanted, nor youthful dalliance as beseems
> Fair couple, linkt in happie nuptial league,
> Alone as they'   (237–40).

The ambiguity is confirmed after Eve's expression of obedience to Adam, when she describes how her first action on
creation was to view herself, Narcissus-like, in a lake. The pleas-
ing shape of her reflection comes and goes with 'looks of sym-
pathie and love' and, even after she has first seen Adam, she
turns back to it until she is recalled by him. The effect is to
suggest an Eve full of self-regard, predisposed, one would think,
despite the stresses on free will, to respond to all flatteries with a
favourable ear, and whose obedience to Adam can be a power
over him and over herself. This is epitomised in the comparison
with Pandora who disseminated evil over the world (714ff).
Dramatic proleptic irony is of course involved; but it is of
doubtful artistic value if it implies criticism of Paradise inadvertently or if we suspect that an extreme and special case is being
used as vehicle of a universal moral.

Then follows the climax of this sensuous first scene:

> 'So spake our general Mother, and with eyes
> Of conjugal attraction unreprov'd,

And meek surrender, half imbracing leand
On our first Father, half her swelling brest
Naked met his under the flowing gold
Of her loose tresses hid; hee in delight
Both of her beauty and submissive charms
Smil'd with superior love . . .' (492–99).

It is not the sensuousness which causes the reader uneasiness but the qualifications and insistent comments. Here, evidently, is a submission and a superiority by which both may be enslaved. But we have already seen Eve's attitude to Adam and acknowledged the fact that she regards him as her 'Guide and Head'; we do not need to be told of 'meek surrender', 'submissive charms', nor, least, of 'superior love'. We have already received more than enough to make us adjust to the fact that physical delights are not to be regarded as remotely shameful in Eden; to be told that the 'conjugal attraction' was 'unreprov'd' is a gratuitous irritant. There is a constant overstatement by means of understatement in these passages which makes us feel that the poet has misjudged his reader who will be aware that what was love before the Fall has potentiality of sinful lust after it.

But of course, this adjustment of the reader to the unfallen world is not the sole point. It is not that Eve goes beyond the ideal even as the language does, but that we are to be left uncertain that she may do, even as Eve causes in Adam a deep anxiety which he recounts to Raphael after the latter has instructed him in the celestial motions. Eve when she first appeared to him, had 'Grace in all her steps, Heaven in her eye' (this reads as a pure lyrical poem), and she was 'not uninformed of nuptial sanctitie'. Again, the double negatives continue:

'though divinely brought
Yet Innocence and Virgin modestie,
Her vertue and the conscience of her worth,
That would be woo'd, and not unsought be won.
Not obvious, not obtrusive, not retir'd,

The more desirable, or to say all,
Nature herself, though pure of sinful thought,
Wrought in her so, that seeing me, she turn'd.'
(VIII, 500–7).

There is, syntactically, half-contradiction between the divine
origin, the virtue, the wooing, the absence of sinful thought.
Adam, no doubt, is surprised to find the divine in origin so soon
humanly orientated, and again we are faced with the ambiguity—Eve's nature is so exceptionally stated either because the
language is misjudged, or because Eve is indeed exceptional,
does indeed go beyond the simpler misconceptions of the require-
ments of paradise. In 'all things else' in Eden Adam finds pure
delight, but the 'commotion strange' of passion seems to chal-
lenge his natural superiority (VIII, 520–33). Perhaps there was
bestowed on her 'too much of ornament, in outward show elaborate'. He knows her to be inferior in 'mind and inward faculties' and resembling God less in image, but in her presence 'all
higher knowledge falls Degraded', and 'what she wills to do or
say Seems wisest, vertuousest, discreetest, best'. Moreover, the
physical attractions create a false platonic image of 'greatness of
mind and nobleness'.

The straight and unhelpful answer to this is that Adam is
weak, and this is the answer Raphael gives. He admits that the
outside is worth 'Thy cherishing, thy honouring, and thy love',
but 'not thy subjection'. But this is none other than Adam has
just said. Raphael adds the suggestion that a higher value set on
Adam's self, an increase in 'self-esteem', will set matters right
and make her acknowledge him her head once more. The 'sense
of touch' is shared with animals and is not 'worthy to subdue/
The soule of Man, or passion in him move'. Then he makes a
distinction between love and passion, 'wherein true love consists
not' and he concludes by blowing the Platonic trumpet loud and
clear:

'Love refines
The thoughts, and heart enlarges, hath his seat

> In Reason, and is judicious, is the scale
> By which to heav'nly love thou maist ascend,
> Not sunk in carnal pleasure . . .'
>
> (589–94).

We seem to be back with 'the bought smile of harlots' again. Adam is 'half-abasht', and well he might be, for Raphael seems not to realise that Adam's love is on his own admission Platonic in the full sense—not a cutting off of the lower rungs of the ladder, but a taking them up with one to the higher levels. Eve's behaviour 'mixt with Love and sweet compliance' in fact declares to him

> 'Union of mind, or in us both one Soule;
> Harmonie to behold in wedded pair
> More grateful than harmonious sound to the ears'
>
> (604–6).

The reader is uncertain whether the earlier sensuous stress represented a contrast with his false imagining of Eden, though a stress somewhat misjudged, or whether Eve is indeed a special threat to Adam. He is unsure whether the picture of love, where Eve regularly admitted her submission to Adam and in which 'youthful dalliance' was emphatically 'not guilty shame, dishonest shame', indicates perfection indeed, or whether Adam was in fact afflicted throughout by the doubts which he now mentions and which the diction earlier led the reader to share. Perhaps Adam's doubts have arisen since that scene and we have not seen their occasion; yet Raphael is delivering this instruction to Adam alone because Eve is meanwhile conforming to the best pattern of wifely obedience:

> 'Her Husband the Relater she preferrd
> Before the Angel, and of him to ask
> Chose rather; hee, she knew would intermix

Grateful digressions, and solve high dispute
With conjugal caresses . . .'

(52–7).

Such is the situation before the separation of Adam and Eve, with the benefit of Adam's comments on it. Do we observe in that separation an instance of Adam's being 'fondly overcome by female charm,' as in the case of his responding to her temptation to eat the apple? Is Eve, in taking up the offer of free will, showing for the first time openly developed the divisive features of her nature which have hitherto, perhaps inadvertently, been suggested?

I think these are possibilities strongly presented to the reader's mind. But they are no more, and the departure of Eve with Adam's consent is no sin on his part or hers, for the emphasis is plain that there is no question of sin and no vestige or predetermination to it before the eating of the apple. One may bear this emphasis in mind and maintain that Milton has kept strictly to such a moral pattern, but in so doing one will have to concede that he has misjudged reactions to the descriptions of love in Eden. I think it would be truer to say that he has enormously complicated things by turning the pattern into a human situation, thereby creating a 'concrete', a dramatically realised, vision of the mystery of ultimate evil more complex than the moral he proposes of obedience to whoever in the hierarchy is most worthy. It is not plain who is most worthy. The situation he creates, in Paradise and after it, is of lovers mutually dependent for their own fulfilment. The relationship of his God and his Man does not parallel this, and the notion of obedience applicable to it, being absolute as God is Absolute, is not the same, although Milton has tried for the sake of his personal myth to make it appear so.

*   *   *

The other element of bias in our attitude to Adam and Eve

arises from Eve's dream in Book V. Here she dreams of eating the forbidden fruit and of wonderful visions which follow. The dream is accounted for by Adam in terms of Reason and Fancy, as we shall see in considering the dream in more detail in connection with *The Faerie Queene*. According to Adam, Fancies, even evil Fancies, may come and go in the mind without harm if unconfirmed by Reason—if the Will, guided by Reason, does not act on them. Though he offers the explanation, he does not seem to regard it as complete. Fancy has 'misjoined shapes' of their 'last evening's talk', but, he admits, there has been 'addition strange' (116). For this addition, the sinister direction of the dream, he offers not explanation but counsel—do not confirm the presence of evil thought by an act of will or it will become actual and not merely potential. It is uncertain whether Eve ate the apple within the dream, though we may possibly assume that she did not; there is a gap between her statement that she 'could not but taste', as she thought, and the vision which she thought she received. The dream is the direct influence of Satan 'squat like a toad' at her ear, but evidently Milton means the parallel between it and the Fall to be of a shadowy nature.

We doubt, I think, that there is so total a breach between waking and dream life as Adam's theory supposes, and in any case we know, as he does not, that the dream is the result of Satan's influence as much as it is due to misshaped memories of the conversation. What we cannot account for, and what Milton does not account for either, is not the various forces Divine and Satanic which are working for and have prescience of the eventual Fall, but the tendency of children who have been told not to put peas up their noses to do so as quickly as possible thereafter. Given an order, the wish to disobey it, of which we see Eve's dream to be a reflection, follows soon after. The assent of the dreaming mind corresponds to a potential assent of the waking mind which has positively to be contradicted by the exercise of will; and it is hard to see how in these circumstances the notions of free will and perfect innocence before the Fall are not to be regarded as in some measure qualified. Again, the human situation which Milton creates is more complex than the pattern to which he would fit it, and it is evident less of a single Fall and a definitive act of the will than of the mysterious nature of evil and the difficulty of deciding when, if ever, that Fall took place.

*   *   *

As the fallen angels are guilty of disobedience rather than of aspiration, but aspiration is their motivating force, so does aspiration creep into the human story of what is at first portrayed as a simple and arbitrary ban. The aspiration is of course primarily to mystical knowledge, but Eve's soliloquy after eating the fruit makes it plain that she does not relish her inferior position to Adam, though for how long this has been so we cannot definitely decide. She is put off from concealing her gains by the thought that she herself may die and Adam be 'wedded to another Eve'; should she

> 'keep the odds of Knowledge in my power
> Without Copartner? so as to add what wants
> In Femal Sex, the more to draw his Love
> And render me more equal, and perhaps
> A thing not undesirable, sometime
> Superior, for inferior who is free?'
>
> (IX, 820–5).

Her faking of dispassionate love for Adam to this end is a terrible thing ('Godhead, which for thee chiefly I sought'), but cannot be allowed to reflect back and influence our judgement of their relationship before the Fall. Yet, as we have seen, Adam's fears for his superiority then are not entirely without basis and what he fears in Eve then is not unrelated to what openly appears in her after she has eaten.

Before the Fall, the appeal of the fruit, apart from that of anything refused, is to knowledge, knowledge perhaps in part as power, but primarily for itself. But this appeal is only gradually

made known to us, and that largely through the probable false-
hoods and certain bias of Satan (and of course the Tree's name).
What powers the trees actually can give Milton skilfully avoids
stating. This Tree is for Adam 'the only sign of our obedience
left' and associated by him with Death, both because of God's
ban and because it is near the Tree of Life. What Death is he
does not know ('some dreadful thing no doubt' (IV, 426))[6] and
does not learn until he witnesses the slaying of Abel (XI, 462).
Satan's overhearing of his speculation permits him to frame his
attack, and it is he who supplies the hubristic theme:

> 'Knowledge forbidd'n?
> Suspicious, reasonless. Why should their Lord
> Envie them that? can it be sin to know,
> Can it be death? and do they only stand
> By Ignorance, is that thir happie state,
> The proof of thir obedience and thir faith?'
>   (IV, 515–20).

Here, on a theme dear to Hegel and common after the eighteenth
century, Satan equates Knowledge with Experience, and leads
the way for those who regard the Fall as an essential birth. God
has previously, unknown to Satan, equated the breaking of this
ban with 'affecting Godhead' (III, 206), but it is Satan who
develops the idea of knowledge specifically in this connection,
and attacks the design

> 'To keep them low whom Knowledge might exalt
> Equal with Gods, aspiring to be such,
> They taste and die'
>   (IV, 525–7),

and he decides on the spot that his temptation will be with
knowledge as the bait, exciting their minds with 'more desire to
know'. Consequently, this attraction looms large in Eve's dream
inspired by Satan, though she goes no further than to have an

airy flight and vision of the 'earth oustretcht immense' below her.

It is not until Book VII, with Raphael's instruction, that the theme enters the poem direct, as distinct from being voiced by a mouthpiece for dramatic purposes. Adam is free, 'though wandering' (the usual pun—cf. VII, 50), and 'yet sinless', but 'led on with desire to know'; there is a definite connection here between sin and infinite knowledge and Raphael elaborates it. He has been told to satisfy Adam's curiosity for 'knowledge within bounds', which is 'what best may serve to glorifie thy Maker, and inferr Thee also happier'. Knowledge is to be limited and moderated, as appetite (VII, 115–30). In his account of the Creation he refers briefly to the ban, but not in connection with hubris (542–7). Adam finds that the account of the War in Heaven and the Creation largely allays his thirst for knowledge, but 'something yet of doubt' remains concerning the vast motions of the universe, and it is at the prospect of a lecture on this that Eve takes herself off to view the gardening, preferring Adam as instructor to Raphael. God, says Raphael, has left these matters largely mysterious, not to 'be scannd by them who ought Rather admire' (73–5). God indeed wishes to have the pleasure of 'laughter at the quaint opinions' of future speculators. Neither Milton nor Raphael has made up his mind whether the universe is in fact geocentric (though the workings of the poem assume it is);[7] either way the system serves man and is to be admired. So Adam is not to 'solicit thy thoughts with matters hid' and to 'think onely what concernes thee and thy being' (167, 174).

As a matter of fact, the dispute does concern Adam's being, since on it depends the relative status of the earth in the scheme of things—is it, as had long been maintained, the hub and direct receiver of all God's benefits downward through the scale of Order, or is it merely one revolving planet among many? This does not, however, affect the status of man as obedient to God, in Raphael's view, and Adam professes himself 'cleard of doubt'. His own account of the ban conforms to that given by God—it is a test of obedience, 'the Pledge of thy Obedience and thy Faith' (VIII, 325). It is the Tree of 'interdicted knowledge' but we cannot tell whether Adam associates the interdiction with the limits set by Raphael.

Limited knowledge is related to limited status and future. Although there are suggestions that man will, after long obedience, reach the heavenly state, his position there is uncertain. Raphael thinks that he may become as the angels, mysteriously and infinitely 'improv'd by tract of time' (V, 498) if he continues obedient. God suggests that man will eventually 'by degrees of merit rais'd' and 'under long obedience tri'd', find his way to heaven, and that there will there be 'One Kingdom, Joy, and Union without end', but this kingdom will doubtless be of the Miltonic order, the only conceivable social order of a potentate and subjects equal by virtue of their true obedience, for only in secure hierarchy is freedom and equality. In power at least Jesus is second rather than first in the poem, and Milton is so firmly on the side of hierarchy that he adopts only rather waveringly the Trinitarian position; God, considering Adam's claim that he is lonely and requires a consort more equal to him than the animals, replies that he, God, is lonely also and does not know 'Second to me or like, equal much less', and he gives Adam a wife inferior not equal. But Milton never commits himself on the issue of the Trinity; in Book III, a book where he is especially careful on points of doctrine, Christ is 'thron'd in highest bliss Equal to God' (305) and yet, shortly afterwards, 'Second to thee' (409).[8]

But, if in the pattern of the poem the potential is firmly limited, it is still to knowledge and aspiration that Satan appeals.[9] In the temptation Eve is first assaulted by a 'wonder', which seems to her to drive a small gap into the system of universal obedience and hierarchy; for beasts to speak 'who God on their Creation-Day Created mute to all articulat sound' indicates either that the low may become high or that the pattern of degree is less universal than she had been given to understand.[10] Ever-ready to draw agreeable inferences, Eve does not doubt that the 'capacious mind' of the serpent, which he evinces by power of speech, is the result of the fruit. Whatever force we give to the previous depiction, we must conclude her coy and acting innocent when she says that his 'overpraising' is so crude as to call in doubt his new access of reason and when she appears not to realise immediately which Tree is concerned; her repetitions of the ban (IX, 647–64) are not those of stupidity or blind obedience, but hesitations, playing for time, awaiting the serpent's next step, which is a masterly and specious oration on the classical theme of hubris.

Still Milton keeps obscure the nature of the knowledge which the Tree might convey (except that it is of the interrelatedness of good and evil), and, at least in a literal sense, Eve's aspirations are fed solely on the evidence that the serpent can now speak and has not died (though, like Adam, she does not know what death is). He appeals not only to aspiration, but to that 'injur'd merit' from which Satan suffered—'shall that be shut to Man which to the Beast Is op'n?' He takes up Adam's first speech on the Tree in the phrase 'whatever thing Death be', and he argues that the death will be of the human as the human becomes as God, just as the death was of the brute as it became human (712). This, ironically, will but reinforce the order subverted, for it will be an elevation preserving the scale of degree, of 'proportion meet'. His arguments are about equally divided between the goodness of knowledge itself and the merits of knowledge in pushing its owner up the ladder.

The decisive point in Eve's thoughts is now that the serpent has not died as, before, it was that the serpent had acquired speech. The temptation to knowledge has made its effect, in part perhaps because she preferred her husband as instructor to Raphael and so missed the angel's warnings against useless knowledge—though Adam doubtless warned his 'weaker' as he was told to do (VI, 908)[10]. But this knowledge, which she does not doubt, will be in vain if followed by death; surely God would not deny knowledge which he has given the brute and also save the brute from death which he has decreed for man?

This is not perhaps a speech (745–779) so much as a pro-jection of Eve's thoughts as she 'muses to herself', and in it are shown clearly the two elements of the Fall, the sense of injured merit at an unjust ban, and the desire to gather what know-ledgeable benefits the fruit has to offer. Eve's reason, her better part, may be overcome, but she is not in any simple sense as yet the victim of irrational passion, however delectable the 'savour' of the fruit may be. It is not until after the first bite that 'greedily she ingor'd without restraint' and became 'hightend as with wine, jocund and boon', 'intent now wholly on her taste', and imagining the taste the best she has ever experienced, because of her 'expectation high Of knowledge, nor was God-head from her thought' (786–93). Immediately after her praise of the sapience of the Tree, she debates, as we have seen, whether or not to share her 'change' and 'happiness', or to retain it for herself and so 'render me more equal . . . for inferior who is free?' (823–5). Then she, like Satan the Orator, greets Adam as an actress, with 'Prologue' and 'Apologie'.

*   *   *

There is no denying that Eve after the Fall is gifted with cunning deception and the full ability to use or abuse her charms—the difficulty is how many of the qualities manifest after the Fall are significantly latent in her before it. She approaches Adam blithely, and the lilt of the rhythm suggests that this is not the continued euphoria and self-deception which descended im-mediately after eating the fruit, but a calculated deceit for a purpose. She affirms that she has missed him and 'thought it long, depriv'd Thy presence', but he has not, to the best of our knowledge, crossed her mind at all save when she wonders whether she would gain or lose by sharing her discovery. She seems to acknowledge guilt in leaving his sight and appeases him with the false claim that she has never felt till now such 'agonie of love' and 'never more mean I to try' going separate from him. She is like someone who, knowing the bank account is dry, goes out and buys an expensive dress, then comes back and says it will last a long time and she will never do it again. She claims to have 'op'ner eyes' and 'ampler heart' as a result of eating. She feels herself 'growing up to Godhead, which for thee Chiefly I sought', which is a ghastly lie. Her repeated appeals to the love which she has violated, if not by the separation most certainly now in spirit, are mingled with a twisted smattering of the obedience and degree theory, when all along we know that her sole motive for sharing with Adam is not love but fear of the consequences of being extinguished alone. How much of the human action in this poem is governed by a consuming fear of loneliness: if it can be ideal, how pernicious also can 'degree' become, whether by voluntary perversion, as Milton seems to suggest, or of its nature as we half suspect:

> 'For bliss, as thou hast part, to me is bliss,
> Tedious, unshar'd with thee, and odious soon.
> Thou therefore also taste, that equal Lot
> May join us, equal Joy, as equal Love;
> Least thou not tasting, different degree
> Disjoine us, and I then too late renounce
> Deitie for thee, when Fate will not permit'
>
> (879–85).

Irony again is large; she would not dream of renouncing deity for him, but, if she has her way, he will renounce Deity for her.

Eve's speech is full of echoes of what should have been, what perhaps was, but what she has instinctively recognised no longer is; there is a hollowness in the repeated 'equal', which shows her appealing to a notion she has rejected—that there was 'equal' love between them, though she was in the position of obedience ('for inferior, who is free?')—and her fear is not that 'different degree' may separate her from Adam, but that she may die alone and be superseded. His reply is not of deception but of love, and it strikes the same note as when he replied to Raphael's Platonic counsel to him on the subject in Book VIII (600–6):

'How can I live without thee, how forgoe
Thy sweet Converse and Love so dearly joind
To live again in these wilde Woods forlorn?'
                                         (IX, 908–10).

Recovered from the initial 'sad dismay', he surveys the arguments—as that the serpent is not dead, that God would not
'destroy us his prime creatures' and that there is a fair chance
that the fruit will give 'proportional ascent'. But they have no
appeal. Adam is unmoved by the temptations to which Eve is
subject. He returns to his unshakeable conviction—

'Our state cannot be severd, we are one,
One flesh; to loose thee were to loose my self.'

If fallen Eve finds these lines 'illustrious evidence' of 'exceeding love' we can be fairly sure that they are meant so only in a
special and limited sense, and that sense is evidently that the
love here displayed is 'exceeding', or, in fact, excessive. That is
not to say that Adam's words are a mockery or that the lyricism
is not genuine; all the evidence is that Milton at this point felt
for Adam in this predicament and intensified it. But we are confronted with the dilemma defined by Waldock; 'the poem requires us with the full weight of our minds to believe that Adam
did right, and simultaneously requires us with the full weight of
our minds to believe that he did wrong.'[11]
    Our reaction here is likely to be governed by our reaction to
the pre-lapsarian scenes. If we have seen in them a perfect love-
situation of which obedience is the essential formal requirement,
we shall tend to reject Adam's submission to Eve here; the love,
like the harmonious kingdom in heaven, lasts as long as the
contract lasts, but it cannot survive the breaking of the contract
and Adam, in supposing that he is acting out of love, properly
understood, must be mistaken—he is acting out of the false
'exceeding love' which is Eve's fallen conception. He has sub-
mitted to her who is not worthiest and love cannot truly survive.

If, on the other hand, we have seen in the situation before the Fall (what is, I think, a juster reading of the lines as they stand) a situation where Adam's dependence on Eve is more than that of lord on servant (in the old sense), and where her dependence on him smacks of a seductiveness which threatens to undermine strict obedience—if, in fact, we have seen a humanly realistic situation poking through the gloss of paradisaical idealism—we shall find Adam's argument both moving and in character. For there will be no stark contrast between his 'love' now and 'love' as it was before.

It is a critical moment. Here undoubtedly are Adam's fears in his discussion with Raphael patently realised. But are we to set against them the stony warning—

> 'For what admirst thou, what transports thee so;
> An outside? fair no doubt, and worthy well
> Thy cherishing, thy honouring, and thy love,
> Not thy subjection'
>   (VIII, 567–70)

or the rejoinder of Adam that this is no transport of the outside that he experiences, but

> 'love
> And sweet compliance, which declare unfeignd
> Union of Mind, or in us both one Soule'
>   (VIII, 603–4)?

Union in love, it seems, there may not be; we sense again the dark loneliness by which God and Adam and Eve are all deeply affected. It is, certainly, a tenable, if a tragic, conception of love, but we cannot easily conclude that Milton or the poem really adopts it. It is the conception which goes with the personal myth of obedience but it is not luminously or consistently held in the poem. To Adam who requires 'fellowship' and 'human consort' to offset his loneliness as a higher being among the animals, God first replies that He also is alone and then jocularly says that this assertion was but 'to try thee, Adam' and arranges for the creation of Eve (VIII, 437). The theoretical answer to Adam's 'How can I live without thee?' is God's 'Seem I to thee sufficiently possest Of happiness, or not?', yet God has granted the imperfection of the parallel between His and Adam's state by giving Adam Eve, and Milton has granted it by being undecided on the substantial worth of the doctrine of the Trinity. When Adam subsequently feels that 'higher knowledge' in Eve's presence 'falls degraded' (VIII, 551), we admit that that is an undesirable state of affairs, but we hardly feel that it indicates an essential and radical fallacy in his love or indeed in human love in general. When he, having considered the pros and cons, and having shown no interest in that aspiration which motivated Eve, decides nonetheless to accompany her for good and ill, the majority of readers surely incline to respect him for a difficult decision manfully taken, for the real alternative as presented in the poem is less God than a rigid system of obedience which is supported by no positive or admirable example.

Adam's love, it may be said, is not selfless; he has not chosen simply between 'Divine displeasure for her sake, or death' (IX, 993), as Eve supposes, but between accompanying her even in sin and what seems the impossibility of living without her. But the love before the Fall is not selfless either; he delights in her obedience and, when he feels in danger of falling into a state of subjection to her, it is not to less, but to more 'self-esteem' that Raphael encourages him (VIII, 572). If there is an ideal love compatible with the loneliness of the obedience theory, it is evidently a love in which selfishness of a special sort plays a considerable part. It is, indeed, hard to conceive of a love which is not a mutual agreement of self-interests and, given the choice, we may reasonably prefer the species which allows some room for giving.

*   *   *

Adam is 'not deceav'd' by argument. He is, however, deceived by the fruit, and shares in the 'fansie' of 'Divinitie within them breeding wings Wherewith to scorn the Earth' (1010), and, whatever the state of sensuousness before the Fall, there is no mistaking the distinction between it and the 'Carnal desire' which 'inflames' them after it. Now Adam 'gan Eve to dalliance move' and we recall that 'youthful dalliance' was one of those aspects of unfallen Paradise which we were to note as 'beseeming' to 'nuptial League' (IV, 338). After the indulgence come the shame and accusations, particularly the accusation by Eve that Adam should never have let her 'wander' and the answer by Adam that to have said more would have been a denial of her free will (1171–4). But he admits that his decision was based on mixed feelings; it was not merely a scruple as to free will, but also that he may have been 'overmuch admiring What seemd in thee so perfect'. The decision he even calls an 'error'. Christ, in his judgement, supports this view of Adam, which was also that of Raphael:

> 'Was shee thy God, that her thou didst obey
> Before his voice, or was shee made thy guide,
> Superior, or but equal, that to her
> Thou didst resign thy Manhood. . . .
>   Adorn'd
> She was indeed, and lovely to attract
> Thy love, not thy subjection . . .'
>   (X, 145–53).

Adam makes a perfunctory hesitation in betraying Eve, and Eve also finds an object outside herself to blame—the serpent. But the serpent was merely the instrument of Satan, who is 'convict by flight' (83), and, being not identified with the evil, is cursed as 'vitiated in Nature' only (169).

The remaining scenes of the Book are concerned with the remorse of Adam and Eve, Adam's despair, and Eve's healing love, which results in Adam's acquiring a more balanced view of things, feeling that God is not without possibility of mercy and prayer may be of some avail. It is, we are told, 'Prevenient Grace descending' from Heaven which removes 'the stonie from thir hearts' (XI, 3–4). What strikes us more is the intervention of Eve. Ironically she takes the initiative, admitting that

> 'both have sinnd, but thou
> Against God onely, I against God and thee
> And to the place of judgment will return'.
>
> (930–2).

It is generous, is indeed a change in Eve's character, but it is a neat formulation rather than the truth. For if Adam sinned against God in eating the fruit, it was not 'against God onely' but against Eve, against the relationship, in the overtrust which, it is claimed, he put in her. And Adam seems to accept this and maintains that she is still misjudging the situation:

> 'Unwarie, and too desirous, as before
> So now of what thou knowst not, who desirst
> The punishment all on thy self'
>
> (947–9).

Should he, superior once in every faculty, the receiver once (presumably) of true obedience and now of an obedience as it were by law ('Hee over thee shall rule' (196)), take any notice of her view? Eve, either under a delusion still or ever incapable of avoiding irony, feels the strength of the argument—

> 'Adam, by sad experiment I know
> How little weight my words with thee can finde . . .'

—and urges that they should now die together. Adam listens, disagrees, and his still 'more attentive mind' rallies to the situation, claims that it is tolerable, and that there is room for prayer. He does not suddenly assert his mastery and regain lost ground over Eve. Rather, he faces life realistically. If it is the product of his superiority still, we surely feel that it is equally the product of the surviving relationship between them both, changed only in degree of frankness and humility, in which each is dependent on, and recognises his or her dependence on, the other. In short, they are free at last of the trammels of a personal myth which came near to destroying their essential humanity.

In Adam's words in this scene where differences are patched up and a common course of action decided, there is a tone we have met intermittently before, and most notably when he considered Eve's suggestion that they separate and she go off gardening on her own (IX, 365–75). Once again Eve's freedom of thought is being considered, and with the same reasonableness. This time she accepts his view rather than his accepting hers. It is not simply a case of Eve's learning from mistakes, or of greater firmness in Adam. That there appears any contrast between this and the earlier situation seems more a datum of plot, governed by the artist's myth, than part of the living drama he has in fact created. We are to suppose that Adam and Eve are now restored on to the right course, which is and will be enforced by the sentence of the Son. But are they? Were they, before the Fall, on the wrong one? Were the criteria by which Adam theoretically fell short in this direction ever relevant to the complexity of human nature, in whatever conceivable state of innocence? The proof of the obedience theory is not whether granted permission, or action without permission, as a subversion of the ideal order, is followed by misfortune, but in whether it destroys the relationship; the relationship is not destroyed, and only to a questionable extent did Adam and Eve exemplify the theory before their Fall.

*   *   *

We have between Adam and Eve two main instances of the personal myth—their separation and Eve's prevailing over Adam to eat the fruit. The situations are different, yet Adam complies with Eve's wish in each, once apparently rightly (though this, as we have seen, is debatable), and once apparently wrongly. Is the difference that Eve is more plainly the temptress and Adam more deeply enslaved by her in the second situation, the eating of the apple? I think not. The situations differ because only in the second one does subverting the rule of obedience on the human level clearly constitute also disobedience to God. The implication, the personal myth, is that the obedience of woman to man and of man to God are closely linked, are the same thing at different stages on the scale of degree and order. But we cannot, surely, accept it; for the relation of the man and the woman, the conception of obedience involved, cannot be the same as the conception of obedience to God exemplified by an unexplained and absolute ban, and the earlier scene of the separation, where Eve was rightly allowed to exercise her free will, has already shown them as different.

For the human level of Milton's poem is realistic fundamentally, and it is perplexingly similar before and after the Fall; Adam and Eve are as much able to face disaster because of their surviving relationship as because of the Prevenient Grace, and that relationship comes most alive in terms of characterisation when the alleged freedom is exercised. The personal myth is a myth in the 'unreal' sense of the word, a pattern which events explode, giving place to a conception of love too complex to be classified in terms of obedience or disobedience, and a conception of sin too mysterious to be pinned down to a precise moment or a particular human failing, much nearer in fact to the obscurity of the original story.[12]

*   *   *

Milton does not, I think, establish the case for a rule of obedience in a human relationship, although he does, almost incidentally, sing the praises of a mutual love wider and more flexible than the rule. Granted that this does not parallel man's (or angel's) obedience to God as urged in the poem, it remains to consider whether the other side of the coin—obedience to God—convincingly transcends arbitrary subservience. Bluntly, I do not see that it does. If Eve has little reason to feel that service is perfect freedom, Satan, or man obeying God, has still less.

The difficulty with Milton's God is that while he stands in a poem ostensibly concerned with an almost mystic sense of obedience consonant with freedom of the will, he himself is found consistently acting against that freedom and resting his justice on the slender and difficult distinction between fore-knowing the course of events and pre-determining it.[13] There *is* some parallel between Adam obedient to God, and Eve obedient to Adam, as there is with Satan obedient to God, but none of these parallels is very close and, while the poem may assert that they *should* be, the reader's reaction is almost bound to be that, from the nature of the characterisation, they could not have been. God gives free will, but he provokes disobedience by setting for man a 'test' which he knows in advance will be failed, although this does not theoretically predetermine that it will be failed. He promotes his Son and this results in the proud disobedience of Satan, yet, when he curiously promotes his Son again, the faithful angels utter an unquestioning Te Deum. Satan, disobeying, in his turn clearly offers a 'test' of character to his lord, to which God is not slow to respond. When Eve 'disobeys' Adam and leaves him she, the 'servant', also offers a 'test' to her lord, but he has not imposed a special 'test' of her obedience on her and we would shrink from the inhumanity of his doing so. It is God who initiates obedience tests, and they belong to the literal sense of obeying or disobeying rules rather than to the complex of dependences enshrined in a living relationship.

There are, of course, difficulties in the story which Milton developed, and they could be surmounted by the assumption that God is always right. But Milton in his portrayal gives grounds more for the notion that might or knowledge is always right, and his God wins by concealing the rules of the game. He thus makes things hard even for the reader predisposed in favour of God.

The poem balances itself between viewing the Fall as a calamity and the other view, more developed in later versions, which sees it as an initiation either into Mercy or into a realm of full Experience after limited Innocence. The calamity was avoidable, but the Mercy was not. As we have seen, Adam finds himself wondering if he should 'repent me now of sin' or 're-joyce much more, that much good thereof shall spring' (XII, 473–6), and it is an open question whether that 'paradise within thee, happier far' (587) is to be preferred either to unfallen Eden or even to that speculated spiritual perfection which Raphael predicted might anyway occur 'improved by tract of time' (V, 498). God has foreseen all this. He knows that 'all this good of evil shall produce' and has even arranged that Death shall be a mercy; the immortality which Adam possessed—independently of the Tree of Life, whose true value is somewhat doubtful ('live for ever, dream at least to live for ever' (XI, 95)[14]—would in the circumstances have served 'but to eternize woe Till I provided Death' (XI, 60–1).

But, though God has foreseen, he has not prearranged:

> 'they themselves decreed
> Their own revolt, not I; if I foreknew,
> Foreknowledge had no influence on their fault'
> (III, 116–8).

We need not join the fallen angels in hell, as they speculate

> 'Of Providence, Foreknowledge, Will, and Fate,
> Fixt Fate, free Will, Foreknowledge absolute,
> And found no end, in wandring mazes lost'
> (II, 588–60),

to feel that Milton, in his portrayal of God and the War in Heaven, has arranged that the tension here shall be fully exploited throughout the poem. Grant the premise that the poem demonstrates eventually the Mercy of God and his bringing good out of evil, and this tension will appear to be justified. Be moved, perhaps unduly, by the magnitude of the disaster of Adam and Eve, and find the compensations as they are presented in the poem less magnificent than either Adam or Michael finds them, and one will doubt the justification.

The distinction emerges most crucially in the sensitive area of the poem from the point of view of the personal myth—the connection between the fate of Satan and the fate of Man, the mechanics of supporting what is to be a thematic connection. The mechanics of prescience are seen first in the ease with which Satan is allowed to enter the Earth to 'pervert' man, 'and shall pervert' (III, 92) because God has foreseen that he will. Uriel is placed as a guard to earth, but is unable to detect the disguised Satan until he overhears his intentions—

> 'For neither Man nor Angel can discern
> Hypocrisie, the onely evil that walks
> Invisible, except to God alone,
> By his permissive will, through Heav'n and Earth'
> (III, 682–5).

Realising his mistake, Uriel mentions his fears to Gabriel, who perfunctorily says that it is 'hard to exclude Spiritual substance with corporeal guard' (IV, 585). There looms over the discussion of Gabriel and Satan the substantial truth of Satan's argument—

> 'Let him surer barr
> His Iron Gates, if he intends our stay
> In that dark durance'
> (IV, 897–9).

To this defiance the angelic squadron retaliate by turning fiery red, with spears as thick, we are told rather oddly (if Homerically), as ears of corn on a peaceful harvest day, and the Almighty, to prevent 'horrid fray', hangs out the scales of Justice, where-

upon Satan, like the serpent, is 'convict by flight'. All this, however, pales before the fact that Raphael, on the sixth day of
creation, was absent from Heaven 'bound on a voyage uncouth
and obscure' to check the defences of hell and 'to see that none
thence issu'd forth a spie' (VIII, 230ff). Raphael visits Adam
on God's order not merely to tell him the limits of useful knowledge, but 'to render man inexcusable' (*Argument*, Book V) by
warning him fully of the propinquity of Satan in the Garden.
This warning in clear terms Raphael never gives, perhaps because to do so would throw more doubt on the uncouth and
ineffectual voyage. Satan cannot leave hell without God's permission and God has his information without the need for an
angelic news-agency. These orders are given and embassies dis-
patched because God did not 'will', yet permitted and fore-
knew, the arrival and victory of Satan. They are claimed to be
'high behests of state' to 'enure Our prompt obedience' (VIII,
240).

To such shifts may the obedience myth be put. There
stands only between the arbitrary and deceitful despot our
assumed belief that whatever God does must, ipso facto, be
good and right. The whole activity is so that Mercy may pre-
vail and the eventual possibly superior 'paradise within' may
be established.

> God,   'in all things wise and just',
>   'Hinderd not Satan to attempt the minde
>   Of man'
>
>   (X, 8),

because with Free Will the mind of man was sufficient to have
stood; yet he sent the angels out on missions in which it was
necessary that they be deceived by Satan and admit their power-
lessness before his deception, and it seems reasonable to suppose
that in respect of deception man was no more proof. The angels
return baffled to Heaven 'much wondering how the suttle Fiend
had stoln Entrance unseen'. God repeats what he had said in

Book III, that the escape of Satan and the Fall are foreknown but in no sense predetermined:

> 'no decree of mine
> Concurring to necessitate his Fall'
>
> (X, 43–4).

Nothing was done to necessitate the Fall, yet little was done to prevent it save for the gift of doubtful freewill. But much was done in terms of Milton's poetic artistry to isolate the act of disobedience from all which precipitated it. It is Milton's strategy to make the forces of necessity too blatant to be used in argument and justification by the self-respecting reader. You cannot say 'Ah, but really he was not free at all!' without appearing rather foolish. The effect is to *defy* us to accept that man was in any way 'excusable' rather than to persuade us gently that he was not. What reason have we to suppose, except that God and the course of myth now wish it, that the 'Cherubic watch' guarding passage to the Tree of Life shall be any more potent than the previous guards of earth and hell (XI, 119–25)?

The other aspect in which doctrine is embodied in technique and mechanics, forcing us to ponder on man's strength and the powers stacked against him, is the handling of the War in Heaven. As there is a constant stress on our credibility of the angelic guards preventing what has been foreseen, so there is a stress on our credibility of a war whose issue is not ultimately in doubt. The effect is to detach this section from the rest of the poem and give us mock-heroic relaxation. Abdiel 'greets' Satan with a colossal blow on his 'impious crest', gives him the heroic equivalent of a punch on the nose. Satan's invention of gunpowder brings a temporary rout to the faithful angels (who might have dodged, as spirits can) and they counter by flinging hills. And yet at times the 'exaggeration', if such it can be called, is less of mock-heroic than of a war threatening the very stability of the universe, good battling with evil in an almost Manichean contest:

'And left large field, unsafe within the wind
Of such commotion, such as to set forth
Great things by small, if Natures concord broke,
Among the Constellations war were sprung,
Two Planets rushing from aspect maligne
Of fiercest Opposition in mid Skie,
Should combat, and thir jarring Sphears confound'

(VI, 309–15).

Milton has it both ways. He produces genuine epic heroics, and yet this war is faked from start to finish. The war is between contestants who were formed 'equal in thir Creation', and it *would* be perpetual Manichean battle but that God has laid the whole thing on for the glory of his Son. The angels, like those sent off as guards, are cheated, yet it is but as an enuring of their obedience again:

'For thee I have ordaind it, and thus farr
Have suffered, that the Glorie may be thine
Of ending this great Warr, since none but Thou
Can end it'

(700–3).

As the rebellion rises, 'nearly it concerns us to be sure of our Omnipotence' . . . 'lest unawares we lose This our high place, our Sanctuarie, our Hill' (720–31); but it is not so—God is joking, as he was joking when he appeared to deny Adam the need for a mate, and there is no doubt that the high place, the sanctuary, the hill will survive:

'Mightie Father, thou thy foes
Justly hast in derision, and secure
Laughst at their vain designes and tumults vain'

(V, 735–7).

For God and the Son are in this together. There is no doubt that the Son will be found to be 'dextrous to subdue' rather than 'the worse in Heav'n' (741–2), but his victory can still receive the full endorsement of Milton's poetry at its grandest (VI, 824–66).

The War has elements of mock-heroic, is won before it is started, not only because the issue is foreknown, but also because this is not in fact where true heroism is to be found. The better fortitude is rather in Abdiel's quietistic obedience to reason, and his furtherance of the notion that Satan is not, as he likes to make out, an eternal evil principle. He was created, Abdiel affirms, like every other angel and, if created, he must be sub-ordinate to his Creator. Satan claims to be 'self-begot' and raised by his own quickening power (V, 860), but, on arrival on earth, he states that God created him what he was in that bright eminence (IV, 43), whilst, by the time of the temptation of Eve, he is again doubting if angels 'are his created' (IX, 145–6). But it is Abdiel's point, to which he sticks throughout, that God 'made thee what thou art' (V, 823) even if Satan thinks it a 'strange point and new' since the angels do not remember their creation.

This argument, on which that of obedience in heaven depends, is the 'better fight', and it is for his maintaining it against all odds that Abdiel is praised as the true servant. Battle will be the 'easier conquest' in comparison. God gives the order to amass forces against those who 'reason for thir Law refuse', but Abdiel remains an example,

> 'for this was all thy care
> To stand approv'd in sight of God, though Worlds
> Judg'd thee perverse'
>
> (VI, 35–7).

Satan, being created by God, owes obedience to God and can be defeated by God—but not yet . . . For a brief spell—for two whole Books—the conventional glories of heroism are both to give delight and to be made ridiculous. And the glories have something else against them; they are the chief condemnation of the Giants of *Genesis* VI, the other version of the Fall from heaven:

> 'Such were these Giants, men of high renown;
> For in those days Might onely shall be admir'd,
> And Valour and Heroic Vertue calld . . .
> Thus Fame shall be achiev'd, renown on Earth
> And what most merits fame in silence hid'
>
> (XI, 688).

But if here, and throughout, there are morally qualified those heroic exploits which caught Milton's poetic imagination, it cannot be said that Abdiel is a strong enough figure to balance them, and in any case the war is not mock-heroic because Abdiel has made war seem petty, but because God has made it needless.

Despite his sense of humour at awkward moments, Milton's God does not live for us as a character, but for the most part as a flat and logical voice largely destitute of imagery. The touches of humour are in fact unfortunate, since they tend to suggest to us that we should be regarding him as a character whose behaviour is able to be assessed in human terms. Nothing can be more fatal than to try to see him in such a light; we may accept that in the facts of life or divine mystery which we would certainly consider monstrous from a human being. Whether we admire the solid austerity of God's main speech (III, 80–134) is perhaps a matter of taste, but certainly it has to be kept as a touchstone of how alone God can be remotely acceptable in the poem, offsetting his later ineptitudes.

The force of intellectual difficulty and justification in the poem comes less from the statements of God than from structural and external devices from which from time to time he has to offer explanation. In this he is like the reader. Often he and the reader know more than any other participant in the action; we know what is happening and then we learn that God knows too; we know what will happen because we have heard this story before, and God knows because he is prescient; we see artistically that the excesses of the War in Heaven are boundless when it comes to throwing hills, and we appreciate God's intervention as a solution to an aesthetic problem as we appreciated its deferment till after the sport; we know the guards will not be any use, and God knows.

But we and God do not know everything at the same time, and our resentment of God is that, when we have made every effort to believe that the guards will work and the war will be an appalling struggle and man will fall (and so on)—he steps in and reminds us that our effort is wasted, there is no suspense, no doubt of the issue. Artistically, he is a killjoy, and thereby, doctrinally at least, he is essential, for he must show that the build-up, the suspense, is all a fake and a misreading on our part. He must throw the 'free' action of Adam and Eve into relief as, apart from the rebellion of Satan, uniquely free and responsible. Poetically, as a story, it is all inevitable, for we accept that as important which has before it preparation leading to inevitable climax, but the duty of that flat voice is to disabuse us of this assumption.

Dramatic irony, in one form or another the key structural device, can make no distinction between foreknowledge and necessity. Milton's constant insistence on the device forces the doctrinal distinction into the limelight. Here is a unique action elaborately prepared for. It must happen—God and history demand it. Here is an everyday action, a simple description reduced to its isolated essential, a matter of disobedience. It need not happen—man has free will. If we can accept the doctrinal distinction, all may be well. But, by his insistence on the device, coupled with occasional slips towards the humanising of God, Milton has left it open to us also to see the doctrine as a means of exculpation for God and man not completely free. Moreover, this may combine with the ambiguities we have noted in Paradise, with the result that we do not feel that the human action entirely fits the pattern which God and the poem suggest.

* * *

The obedience of man to God and of man and woman are not, and Milton does not convince us that they could or should be, the same thing, though the system of order and degree supposes that they are. Adam, lacking in self-esteem, and falling unwittingly into what seems perfect love, but what Raphael regards as a 'transport of the outside', Adam granting a reasonable wish to Eve, is not strictly comparable with God, who sets exercises to demonstrate the disaster of exercising free choice in a direction of which he disapproves. Obedience absolute may be owed to God, but Milton does not convince us that it is truly consonant with free will. Obedience of man and woman we do not see unambiguously. What we seem to see rather is a situation of harmonious mutual dependence which, when it is broken, results in catastrophe, but catastrophe conceivably recoverable as much through the survival of that love as through Prevenient Grace.

There run through the poem three strands—the bare biblical story, the Miltonic associations of divine and human obedience, and the living relationship of Adam and Eve, questionably paradisaic at first, frankly fallen at last, but nonetheless noble in its survival. In both the last two, the personal myths of the poem, we find the idea of the Fall as an ordinary act, such as may be repeated, from which man will recover, by his efforts, by love, by Grace, and knowing increasingly good and evil not by themselves but in terms of each other.[15] Milton chose to pit against themselves the external poetic treatment of God and his Angels, and the dramatic, humanly moving treatment of Adam and Eve. The argument as such of the personal myth does not work, but its failure is what lives for us.

PART II

The Way of the Developed Story

3. The Old English *Genesis B*

'By Fallacy surprised'—Milton.

The Old English *Genesis* represents the 'developed story' in as pure a manner as we shall find it in considering versions of the Fall. It is at one extreme where Romantic versions and *Lord of the Flies* are at the other. As a result, a certain caution is necessary. For example, if we could find a source for the Old English work rather closer than the biblical version, we might very easily conclude that in his departures from this source and his additions to it the poet displayed his originality, and that what merit lay in these departures would be a large part of the merit of the whole work. This does not follow in theory or in practice, but it has enough truth in it to be tempting. Again, taking the biblical version as the basic myth, and emphasising in the modern way the poem's substantial unity, its fusion of form and content, together with its apparent addition of a dramatic structure to join the goings-on in heaven and hell with the goings-on in earth, we might conclude that here was a curiously modern poem in which sources and their study could be cast to the winds and the retrospective and fundamentalist stance of the poet might be happily disregarded. This would not do either. The difference between developed story and personal myth is certainly one of degree, but it seems to me quite clear that the Old English poem lies much nearer to one end of the scale than to the other. Its superiority to related versions is not due solely to whatever of personal myth it may possess, though certainly that element is among its distinctions.

The poem, it is generally agreed,[1] is composed of two large fragments, of different date, style, and even thought, though ostensibly concerned with the same subject, the later fragment, known as *Genesis B,* being roughly inserted into the other. *Genesis A* (being lines 1–234 and 852–2936 of the whole) dates probably from the end of the seventh or beginning of the eighth century, and *Genesis B* (235–851) is probably a century later. Brief study of a commentary on the biblical story will show that that also is a combination of fragments with the edges not entirely smoothed over. In both cases, no doubt, the fragments were felt to be equally inspired, in periods when little of the largely vocal art of poetry was permanently recorded, and on the same theme, and so they were pieced together.

But, although they are incomplete, we can form some idea of the different structures proposed for the two Old English works. They are most clearly seen when tabulated:

Genesis A $\left\{\begin{array}{l}\text{The Fall of the Angels} \\ \text{The Creation}\end{array}\right.$

Genesis B $\left\{\begin{array}{l}\text{The Ban on the Tree} \\ \text{The Fall of the Angels} \\ \text{The Fall and Judgement of Man}\end{array}\right.$

Genesis A   Continuation

Without going into details, we can see that the starting with the Creation of Man (most probably) and certainly with the Prohibition, leads to an account based on human realities and, within its limits, may produce some psychological interest. Further, it leads to a direct juxtaposition of the two Falls. For the modern reader, by contrast, the *Genesis A* fragment appears to stick to the chronological order. It was not for the poet necessarily a chronological order, because whether or not the creation of man preceded the rebellion in heaven (and whether it was the part motivation for that rebellion) was a much debated question;[2] but, however this may be, this poem would evidently have separated the two Falls by the Creation and followed the biblical account of the Fall of Man fairly closely, whereas the later poet, by placing the Falls together, exploits parallels between them and forms an individual staging for the human drama. In *Genesis B* the prohibition is followed by the Fall of the Angels and only then by the Fall of Man. As we have it, this is a very effective opening 'in medias res', into the midst of things, but of course the opening is incomplete and was most probably preceded by the Creation. Nevertheless, the separation of ban and Fall must always have produced the interest of dramatic suspense which it now has. These were bold moves and they put us at the outset onto a higher level of artistry than we find for the most part in *Genesis A*.

Milton's scheme is no less bold and similarly does not offer a plain sequential narrative. He manages to have the advantages of both schemes. Starting with 'the prime cause of his Fall, the Serpent, or rather Satan in the Serpent' in hell, he leaves the reasons for Satan's Fall and the account of the rebellion to be narrated in Book V, and the Creation after it in Book VII; thereby he is able first to define the perspectives Satanic and Divine against which the human action will take place, while still arranging that the War in Heaven and Fall of Satan directly precede (though as narrated by Raphael) the Fall of Man. This arrangement is not only sufficiently startling; it also makes us compare, as the personal myth requires, several impressions of related events.

*   *   *

Not only the whole structure as we may imagine it, but also the Fall of the Angels is entirely different in conception and treatment in the two Old English fragments. The two versions are in fact incompatible in detail and both make it impossible for us to view them even loosely as one work and reflect the superior art of the poet of *Genesis B*.

Both versions lay emphasis on pride[3] as the principal cause of the rebellion, but *Genesis B* is at pains to fill in the narrative detail and to make of Satan a plausible rival lord of the Germanic tradition, whilst suggesting also the theme of hubris which is to play a part (in this case a peculiarly subtle part) in the Fall of Man—'Ic maeg wesan god swa he' (283—I may be God as well as He). Although *Genesis A* naturally uses the terms of warfare, its Satan does not speak as a general—indeed, he does not speak at all—whereas the later Satan consistently does so:

> 'Bigstandath me strange geneatas, tha ne willath me aet
>   tham strithe geswican,
> haelethes heardmode. Hie habbath me to hearran gecorene,
> rofe rincas; mid swilcum maeg man raed gethencean,
> fon mid swilcum folcgesteallan'
>
> (284–7).

> ('Brave comrades stand by me,
> Stout-hearted heroes unfailing in strife.
> These fighters fierce have made me their leader;
> With such may one plan and muster support.')[4]

It is on the heroic fidelity, the spirit of 'comitatus', of the men to their chosen leader ('hearran') that Satan relies in estimating the prospects of his campaign, and it is the infidelity of that leader to the supreme leader (again, 'hearran'—294) which incenses God. This parallel and contrast—one of the several woven into the poem—doubtless underlies *Genesis A*, as indeed some sort of parallel appears in many versions which include a Fall of the Angels, but it is less constantly or forcefully suggested to us.

Genesis A is concerned with the presentation of fact as it was thought historically conceivable, we may assume. *Genesis B* is concerned rather with imaginative impact and what can be made of the fact. The poet's means of achieving the impact is the arrangement of his structure and his realisation of its potential through the role of Satan. 'Satan' is named as the leader of the angels, a heroic person, yet it is also contrived that he shall be a mysterious and impersonal agency of evil. A combination of circumstances now impossible to unravel has arranged that Satan himself shall not perform the temptation of

Man or be identified with the Serpent.[5] He, bound in hell, is distinct from the 'messenger' who performs in Eden, and the messenger is further distinct from the serpent into which he for a time enters. Obviously there is an important sense in which Satan *is* present at these events, but the blending of traditions and the artist's skill have arranged that he shall be felt primarily as an evil influence—and this despite his very human characterisation in heaven and in his speech from hell.

In *Genesis A* the creation of the world is undertaken specifically as a consolation for the loss of the fallen angels:

> 'The theohtede theodan ure
> modgethonce, hu he tha maeran gesceaft,
> ethelstatholas eft gesette,
> swegltorhtan seld, selran werode,
> thaet hie gielpsceathan ofgiffen haefdon
> heah on heofenum'
>
> (92–7).

> ('Then our Lord pondered how to people again
> With a better host His ample creation,
> The native settlements and sunbright seats
> High in heaven whence the insolent angels
> Had been driven out.')

In *Genesis B*, by contrast, we have already seen Adam, and, whenever he was actually created, all is directed to intensifying the relation of man and the angels:

> 'Thaet me is sorga maest
> thaet Adam sceal, the waes of eorthan geworht,
> minne stronglican stol behealdan,
> wesan him on wynne, and we this wite tholien,
> hearm on thisse helle'
>
> (364–8).

('Tis my greatest sorrow
That Adam, fashioned and formed of earth,
Should hold my high seat and abide in bliss
While we suffer this torture, this torment in hell.')

In *Genesis A*, that is, the relation of Satan and Adam is solely in the mind of God (and the reader), whilst in the later poem it is carefully placed in the soliloquy of Satan and an important element in his changing from despair to action. In the first place the 'heofonrice', the heavenly kingdom, is something for which Satan and Adam are rivals (386–8), and which Satan still values. In the second place it is a case of sour grapes—since he is bound and the kingdom of heaven is not available to him—

'Uton othwendan hit nu monna bearnum,
thaet heofonrice, nu we hit habban ne moton, gedon thaet
hie his hyldo forlaeten,
thaet hie thaet onwendon thaet he mid his worde bebead'
(403–5).

('Since we may not regain it
Let us wrest heaven's realm from the sons of men
Make them forfeit His favour, break His command.')

Then not only will Adam be deprived of the kingdom, but the kingdom itself will lose its true nature, will no longer be peopled with pure souls (397). The fact that God had foreseen this development (385) is responsible for Satan's being bound, and therefore the direct cause of the complexity of the Temptation arrangements, which Satan himself cannot effect. The poet does not worry that Satan should not be able to get out of hell. He arranges for no ineffective angelic guard like that of Milton's poem. It is, perhaps, more conceivable that the agent, rather than the devil himself, should be able to pass through the barriers; there is a passage missing here, and we move suddenly from Satan to messenger, whose recruitment or volunteering we do not see, but the whole approach of the poet makes it seem unlikely that he would be greatly worried by the difficulties that Milton found.

Summarising the poem's originality, we may say that it is essentially dramatic, whether we find drama in the use of the 'messenger', in Satan's soliloquy, in the simple comments which (though not entirely) replace with poignant irony the age's tendency to direct preaching of a moral, or in the manipulating of the ideas of a heroic society in the War in Heaven. The opening ends characteristically with a foreboding comment, in itself of no great subtlety, but which combines with other instances of the device to suggest inevitability in the course of events. 'Heo waeron leof gode thenden heo his halige word healdan woldon' —they were dear to God whilst they kept His word. And then we leave Adam and Eve and are plunged straight into the idea of obedience which is defined in heaven.

God gave Satan certain gifts, and he therefore expected certain fidelity in return, as the lord expects fidelity of his thegn —this simple code is the basis of heroic society, and therefore, for the time, applies equally to Satan and to Adam and Eve. There is no need for subtlety of debate on foreknowledge and predestination. These can be implied by the statements of narrative and relationship; since 'he was dear to our Lord', it follows that 'ne miht him bedyrned weorthan/thaet his engyl ongan ofermod wesan' (261—'nor long was it hid that his angel was growing ungrateful and bold'). It is accordingly no error of judgement which allows God to dispense gifts and favours and seems to us to precipitate and encourage the pride of Satan. The poem accepts the code of heroic society, the distribution of rewards and incentives which are not felt necessarily to corrupt. Hence Satan, though having striven to erect a rival throne in heaven and then preventing Adam and Eve from enjoying the heavenly kingdom he has lost, continues to view the hall, with its lord and servants, as a positive and desirable object and a viable system, even though he has violated the allegiance on

which it must be based. He is not a machiavellian prince enlarging an empire and jealous of rivals, but the original violator
of a mystical relationship continually celebrated in Germanic
poetry; he is a threat to civilised society. In Milton's poem the
situation is rather different; the ideal system, theoretical as it
may seem, is found in heaven and Satan's system in hell is without its essential merit. In *Genesis B* Satan, though having broken
the relationship in heaven, yet sets up an alternative hell
apparently indistinguishable in concept, though of course a
parody and mockery by reason of his straitened circumstances.
Proposing to build his hall in the west and north of heaven (276),
he does so ('trymede getimbrod'), but alas the north-west is also
the direction of hell.[6] His 'gylpword', his heroic boast, common
to the successful as well as the braggart warrior in this poetry, is
mocked by understatement—'cwaeth him tweo thuhte/thaet he
gode wolde geongra weorthan' (276—'he said that he doubted
he would serve god', it seemed to him doubtful whether he
would be God's companion in arms). Certain that 'Ic maeg
wesan god swa he' ('I can be a god as well as he'), he yet
depends on the allegiance of his 'strange geneatas', his trusty
companions, to realise the boast. The account of the Fall of Satan
is of the realising of the letter of this boast without its spirit. He
builds his hall and has his band of followers and, in a limited
sense, he keeps Adam and Eve from that earthly kingdom
modelled on the heavenly of which he is jealous. The pattern is
simpler than Milton's; Milton has an elaborate scheme of
obediences, of Satan to God, of man to God, of woman to man,
and less close parallels between God's system and Satan's, than
has the Old English poet.

In Satan's great soliloquy in hell, which is at the heart of this
section of the poem, he gradually evolves an attitude and a plan
which will justify the letter of his claims in heaven and destroy
as far as possible the evidence outside heaven that there is a
'heofonrice', a spiritual state transcending his own external
system of obedience and reward. In the Old English *Christ and
Satan*, Satan laments his fall and his angels defy him and accuse

him of broken promises. The boast of establishing a faithful hall
is not fulfilled and this is an additional mental torture. But in
Genesis B, after the initial characteristically hard-headed summing up of the situation by understatement ('Is thaes aenga
styde ungelic swithe/tham othrum ham the we aer cuthon'—
'Unlike indeed is this narrow land/To that other home that of
old we held') and the admission that they were unable to defend
their kingdom in heaven, Satan himself is immediately defiant
and confident of the support of his men. In fact, it is his ambition
not only to deprive man of his heavenly kingdom but also to
enlist him in his own ranks 'to giongrum', as followers. It is the
recurrent thought of the creation of Adam, destined to inherit
his place in the heavenly kingdom, which brings about positive
advances towards his ultimate plan:

> 'Thaet me is sorga maest
> thaet Adam sceal, the waes of eorthan geworht,
> mine stronglican stol behealdan . . .'

> (364-8).

> ('Tis my greatest sorrow
> That Adam, fashioned and formed of earth,
> Should hold my high seat and abide in bliss
> While we suffer this torture, this torment in hell').

But this jealousy and his previous sense of the injustice of God
in imposing a torment more severe than the disgrace of defeat
are for the present rendered impotent by the fact that he is bound
and immobile. The progress of the speech at one level is from a
state where this obstacle is viewed as total to a state where it
counts for nothing. The progress is achieved by launching an
appeal—as in Milton's version—to his followers, an appeal
which (in contrast to Milton's version) by the end he is certain
will be met. Though there is missing from the poem a section
where (presumably) a volunteer steps forward, it seems that
Satan's ability to call on a deputy reflects a more successful

imitation hall and company than the angels in *Paradise Lost* could compose.

Pondering upon the severity of his punishment and the assurance that, being bound by both hands and neck,[7] he cannot move, he calls to mind that this particular punishment was ordained by God in foreknowledge that Satan's attempt in his apostasy would be to deprive Adam of the kingdom which he himself had lost (378-9). Throughout, there is a distinction between this 'heofonrice' and the smaller kingdom which he and his angels were unable to retain when they set up a hall apart from that of God; the former is a value which Satan did not fully realise before his Fall.

Again he returns in frustration from this thought to his own imprisonment and comes back yet again to the creation of earth and Adam. This third contemplation of the subject is accompanied by a richer realisation of what he has lost and what God by Adam plans to gain, or what Adam stands to gain (for the application of 'him' in line 400 is uncertain):

'He haefth nu gemearcod anne middangeard, thaer he haefth
    mon geworhtne
Aefter his onlicnesse. Mid tham he wile eft gesettan
Heofena rice mid hluttrum saulum'

(395-7).

    ('He has marked out the margins of middle-earth
    And created man in his own image
    By whom to repeople the plains of heaven
    With pure souls.')

Now the idea that Adam and God must be deprived of their desires so dominates him as to break the circle of thought which previously returned him from Adam to his own impotence. As the climax of his self-assertion he affirms what his jealousy of Adam (which seems to be both envy at being supplanted and

antipathy to God's extending his kingdom) shows clearly to be
untrue:

> 'Ne gelyfe ic me nu thaes leohtes furthor thaes the he him
>   thenceth lange niotan,
> thaes eades mid his engla craefte'
>
> (401–2).

> ('No longer have I any hope of that light
> That he thinks long to enjoy in bliss
> With his angels.')

He accepts indeed fully, perhaps for the first time, that he cannot hope to regain 'that light'. But his describing it so, and his
preceding words, as well as his repeated insistence that it is
unobtainable, show that he regards it as more than ever desirable and to be valued. This gain of awareness at the expense of
indefinable bliss—as a later poet may lament the clouds of
glory whence he came, or the bliss of infancy from which he falls
to maturity—is a theme of repeated importance in versions of
the Fall, and of course it is paralleled by the backward regard
of Adam and Eve to Paradise, the knowledge of good by evil
supplanting that of good in itself.

Thus Satan deceives himself. Defiantly he declares he no
more can accept the value (an alternative reading) of what his
very words declare him to value more fully than ever. In this
new position an important detail of the plan first occurs to him
—that breaking God's command about the fruit shall be the
way to deprive Adam of the heavenly kingdom (405) and to add
him and his descendants to his own number. With unconscious
irony at his own response to the 'lean' (the gift or reward) of
God, Satan proceeds to suggest that his angels may now suitably
repay him for those gifts which he formerly bestowed on them
'on tham godan rice' by flying out of hell and depriving man of
the riches which should be theirs in heaven, for, yet again,

'Thaet me is on minum mode swa sar
on minum hyge hreoweth, thaet hie heofonrice
agan to aldre'

(425–7).

('My soul is sorrowful, my heart is sore
That they should hold the heavenly realms for ever.')

It is fortunate indeed that he has the memory of gifts bestowed in heaven available as a reward, for, as he wryly observes (437–8), he has in the present situation nothing to offer man but the symbolic pleasure of sitting beside him in the fires of hell.

This soliloquy is a remarkable achievement. In it we are presented with the motives for the Fall of Man, shown more fully the heroic themes adumbrated before, and given a living study at once in defiance and progressive corruption. It is, of course, a portrayal of defiance against desperate odds, but, in that the odds in this version are not entirely victorious (for this is not, as we have it, a version complete with Christian consolation), and in that Satan seems partly to recognise the value of what he sets out to destroy, it is not a simple conception of evil that Satan represents—and this is seen further in the human Fall.

*   *   *

As the Fall of the Angels is distinguished particularly by the dramatic conception of Satan's soliloquy, by the end of which he is again proposing to wrest a kingdom from its lord, so the handling of the Fall of Man is marked by the dramatic conception of an action overlooked. First we are conscious of the initiator of the action bound in hell and awaiting a report from his minion that it has been successfully undertaken, and secondly this is reinforced by the hellish messenger's standing aside and watching the working of his poison as Eve labours all day to persuade Adam to join her and eat the fruit (684ff). Once she has succeeded in this (in which he, Satan's emissary, has previously failed) he gives thanks to his lord and returns gleefully to hell (723ff).[8]

Originality concerns the exploitation of sources rather than independence from them. In the Fall of Man it will seem novel to the modern reader that the staging of the temptation is governed by the fact that Satan is bound in hell, and the introduction of a messenger who is further distinct from the serpent (so that, in a sense, we have the powers of evil split three ways) will seem still more curious.[9] But the poet, though certainly exercising a vigorous imagination, has exploited suggestions already present in less well-known traditions of the Fall, traditions which either in origin predate the identification of Satan and the serpent or seek to explain an identification already made. In the *Vita Adae et Evae*[10] (probably composed between the second and fourth centuries A.D.) Eve, doing penance by standing up to her neck in the River Tigris, is visited by Satan in the guise of an angel, who assures her that her penance is sufficient. She is taken in by him, and it is Adam who reveals the angel's true nature. Unmasked, Satan explains his animosity to man by an account of his own Fall, which arose from his proud refusal to bow down to the newly created man when Michael ordered him to do so. The *Apocalypsis Mosis*[10] (which is probably rather earlier) gives an account by Eve of how her fall came about, in which are a number of features which it is not clear how she came to know about but which are of some relevance to the Old English *Genesis*. The devil approaches the serpent, as the wisest of the creatures, and persuades it to act as the 'vessel' of his words. There follows a curious double conversation in which Satan speaks first as an angel to Eve, when she sees him singing hymns, and then, concerning the fruit, through the mouth of the serpent. He has not made any previous attempt on the virtue of her husband, but he insists before she eats that she first swear to make Adam do so afterwards. He overcomes her indeed partly by deception—but it is mainly because she is ready to accept the offer of godlike knowledge that she is deceived. Such knowledge she is said to receive, a knowledge particularly of shame (for Satan has previously poured the poison of lust on the fruit), and which turns out to be unwelcome, just as Satan's new realisation of what has been lost is tainted by a corrosive bitterness in *Genesis B*.

It is hard to believe that these versions do not represent traditions widely current, which contributed to Eve's being tempted by an angel who is only ambiguously Satan and serpent in the Old English poem. Yet the differences are marked and, for this poem, crucial. Whilst in the *Apocalypsis* Eve is apparently deceived as to the nature of her tempter, his temptation is framed in terms clearly opposed to God's wishes. There is no attempt at all to suggest that, as in *Genesis B*, God has issued a new command that, after all, the Tree may be eaten, or, further, that God will follow close on the angel's heels and upbraid Adam and Eve if they have not eaten it. On the contrary, the angel plainly states that God imposed the ban lest, having eaten of the fruit, Adam and Eve should acquire a measure of divinity; this is of course the more widely current version which even Milton follows, and the Old English poet's departure from it seems to represent the domination of fictional and dramatic interest in his mind over the normal theme and situation with which he surely must have been familiar. Furthermore, if this poet was influenced by the *Apocalypsis* and *Vita Adae et Evae* traditions, he has avoided the difficulty of having Eve give an extended account of her fall (a difficulty which as we have seen, for his own thematic reasons, Clough turned to advantage in his Mystery of the Fall).

Again, in his handling of the apparent confusion of the two Trees in the biblical account,[11] the Old English poet shows a readiness to let clarity of story and dramatic contrast be guiding motives. The tradition (mainly in the *Books of Enoch*) on which the poet drew for his Fall of the Angels usually either omits the Tree of Life altogether or locates it in a different part of the Garden. But the Old English writer, whether on his initiative or by use of another tradition, opposes the two Trees rather than leaving them unrelated, for he has a Tree of Life and a Tree of Death (which is also that of Knowledge), but although both Trees appear in the manuscript illustrations, he has omitted the Tree of Life from his account of events after the Fall. No source has been discovered for the description of the Trees here, and there is no reason to suppose that there was one. It develops the simple antitheses of early Christian poetry and the disastrous consequences of this fruit.

The nature of the tempter, besides playing its part in the dramatic structure of the poem, has also a bearing on its conception of evil and the nature of the crucial act. In line 491 the Satanic messenger enters the body of the serpent, of whom nothing else is said, and with whom he is identified. It is grammatically the angel in the serpent's body, and not merely the serpent, which 'wand him tha ymbutan/thone deathes beam thurh deofles craeft' (492—'wound himself around the tree of death by devilish skill'), and it is he, not Eve, who plucks the fruit (cf. *Paradise Lost*, IX, 590ff, where Satan the serpent winds round the trunk and plucks the fruit which the other animals cannot reach and, though he says it would require the 'utmost reach' of Adam or Eve, Eve seems to reach it without difficulty. In the *Apocalypsis*, the serpent bends the bough so that it can be reached.) The 'serpent' thus participates in the crime directly. He is referred to in terms used equally of Satan himself—he is 'se latha' ('the evil one'), with a devil's cunning ('feondes craeft'). As an angel, presumably, and possibly reflecting some current dramatic representation anticipating the disguises of Mystery plays, he indicates some oddity of appearance that 'ne eom ic deofle gelic' ('I am not like a devil'), yet it is with 'wyrmes getheaht' that she begins to yield (590). Repeatedly he is 'se sceatha', 'se forhatena', the accursed. Serpent, angel, Satan, and even Eve, become curiously mingled and this prepares us for Eve's admission of her total deception, where she has no doubt that he is an angel ('ic on his gearwan geseo/thaet he is aerendsecg uncres hearran'— 657–8. She can see by his dress that he is a messenger from God), and reminds us of that comparison of the heavenly and hellish kingdoms which pervades the Fall of the Angels.

Thus we are given a situation which appears dramatically controlled by the absent Satan. We perceive that the success of his plan will depend on the success of the disguise and the allegiance of his messenger, and it is also suggested that there is a third ramification of the idea of faithful obedience as seen in the relations of Adam and Eve. For, whilst the analysis has none of the complication, or indeed the moral intention, of Milton's, it cannot escape us that Eve is overcome by deception as much as by temptation, and that that deception is to be attributed as much to the sheer stupidity of woman in the poet's scheme as to the nature of the angelic disguise, and of this stupidity Adam is insufficiently aware. Free will, the doctrinal theme, is sub-ordinate here to an artistic conception in which deceit will win. It may be thought that the powers of foreknowledge observed in Milton's poem constitute impossible odds, but they are small compared with the novel handling here, and, if free will appears compromised, the mysterious and incalculable origin of evil is in some ways more simply and more fully realised by the simple device.

The angel's approach to Adam is notable for the paralleling of the situations in heaven and hell which has already been men-tioned. Satan offered to the successful thegn permission to sit with his lord (438), and the angel now announces that his journey is ordered by God, with whom he has lately been sitting (498–9). All this, unbeknown to Adam, reflects ironically on the actual nature of the angel and his lord:

> 'Nele that earfethu
> sylfa habban thaet he on thysne sith fare,
> gumena drihten, ac he his gingra sent . . .'
>
> (513–5).

> ('He does not wish to have the hardship
> Of making this journey but sends his servant.')

His appeal is to any ambition in Adam which may have been raised by God's description of the Tree's powers (not in the extant fragment). The temptation is to obey an order of God and accept the 'help' which, it is claimed, God has offered. This 'help' is itself ironical, seeming to refer to the 'grace' which was to be an aid against the pernicious consequences of the Fall, and Eve goes on to say that Adam will need the 'hyldo' of the messenger, as if the satanic messenger has any grace to offer (664).

Adam's response is so pious and rigid as to be dramatically implausible—it is a datum, rather like the stupidity of women, which scarcely fits the situation created. God has evidently given more warning about the Tree than appears in the scriptural account, has mentioned it as a potential deceit, and advised that those who perform evil will dwell in 'dark hell', a notion which can have meant little more than 'death' does to Milton's Adam, but nonetheless Adam's mind appears more closed and rigid than can have been wished from the story's point of view, although we may suppose he has his function as showing allegiance solely to his Lord and, by subsequent behaviour, putting Eve above that allegiance. We learn further that whilst Adam could fairly complain that the angel showed him no 'tacen' or proof that he came from God, he did produce such identification for Eve (540, 653).[12]

The angel's temptation of Eve follows different lines. If she does not obey his command, something very like Original Sin, or at least hereditary evil, will afflict her children, when in fact precisely this is going to follow her yielding to him. He is sarcastic, mocking any thought in Eve that an order at second hand will not do:

> 'He only, forsooth,
> Must come to instruct you; His messengers
> May not tell you his bidding . . .!'
>
> (558–60).

He and she will get together and work on Adam, and then she will have power over him and he will cease to disobey God with rude answers—

> 'he thone lathan strith,
> yfel andwyrde an forlaetath
> on breostcofan, swa wit him bu tu
> an sped sprecath'
>
> (572–5).

('He will cease this evil strife, these evil answers,
As we both shall urge him to his own good.)

Then the poet characteristically ends with dramatic irony, appealing to the reader over and above the speaker's immediate audience—

> 'Ac ic cann ealle swa geare engla gebyrdo,
> heah heofena gehlidu; waes seo hwil thaes lang
> thaet ic geornlice gode thegnode
> thurh holdne hyge, herran minum,
> drihtne selfum; ne eom ic deofle gelic'
>
> (583–7).

('Yet I know full well
All the angel orders and heaven's high span,
So long was the time I served my lord
With loyal heart. I am not like a devil.')

At this climactic moment direct comment is introduced—in a manner not really sympathetic to modern taste. We are told that God assigned to woman a weaker mind but also what is in a way distinctive of this version with its stress on deception— deception is a fact and the desire for knowledge is a fact, and they issue, and seem bound to issue, in disaster. There is this ambiguity about the poem as a version of the Fall, and it distinguishes it both from Milton's argumentative, justificatory version, and from the biblical source with no questions asked; although it is in form and conception dramatic, its burden is essentially elegiac and the imperfection of the scheme of things is a matter for wonder. It is towards this elegiac note that the moralistic comments are directed and, if read in this sense, they are less intrusions than enlargements of the poem; it is not so much a story with 'moral', as a drama with lyrical notes.

> 'Thaet is micel wundor
> Thaet hit ece god aefre wolde
> theoden tholian, thaet wurde thegn swa monig
> forlaedd be tham lygenum the for tham larum com'
> (595–8).

('Great is the wonder that Eternal God
Would ever permit so many of his servants
To be tried with lies that came as good counsel.')

This is reinforced by the following lines. It is not that Eve failed to acquire knowledge from the fruit but that the knowledge she did acquire, although accurate and a positive revelation, was as a light too bright for human vision, knowledge unfit for the limited state of human beings even in Paradise. To Eve in fact it seems that heaven and earth are more beautiful and the work of God greater (603–5) not than they in fact are, but than they had previously seemed to be. To see the nature of heaven and earth as God sees them is too much for man to bear. This is not a notion present in the scriptural version and it is one of the distinctions of the poet that he is at some pains to make it clear. The vision of God and his angels in the south-east, which she recites to Adam as evidence of the fruit's benevolence, may well be understood as sadly real. But 'human kind cannot bear very much reality', and the same intoxicated happiness leads her to confuse the messenger of Satan with one of these heavenly angels. Therefore it is with special 'feondscip' that he can point out how she was profited by eating the fruit and tell her to pass on the good news to Adam, assuring her that his 'womcwidas' (Adam's rude reply to the temptation) will be erased from the debit account and his children not after all be afflicted.

The irony is poignant. Eve, overlooked by the messenger, spends the whole day persuading Adam and eventually he gives in. Partly it is her radiance, for this Adam is overcome by female charm, but more particularly it is that Eve's vision of heaven and angels rings true, is indeed true. She persuades him because she is convinced that she is acting as a missionary. She is acting God's will and converting Adam who has already, as she sees it, disobeyed Him.

Immediately he eats, a tension is released. The serpent is forgotten and the messenger sheds his disguise and capers about like a buffoon, giving his lord consolation for his torments in the assurance that man will soon be with him in hell:

> 'Swa thus his sorge ne thearft
> beran on thinum breostum, thaer thu gebunden ligst,
> murnan on mode, thaet her men bun
> thone hean heofon . . .'

> (733–6).

> ('So you need not languish lying in bondage,
> Or mourn in spirit that men shall swell
> in heaven on high . . .')

He claims indeed that both Satan's desires are now realised; but, though God suffers 'hearm' and 'modsorg', he does not, as Satan seems to expect, forthwith cast man into hell and only in a very partial sense has Satan won man for his kingdom and deprived him of the 'heofonrice'.

Whether Adam or Eve hears any or all of this speech is not clear, but they see his light fading as he returns to hell and they know they are victims of a deception. The exact nature of their immediate misery is convincingly uncertain. It is perhaps partly the effect of the fruit's poison working within them. They realised that God's command had been broken, or, in an alternative translation, they thought (at the time of eating) that his command had been reversed. They pray together and invite God's punishment. Realising for the first time their nakedness, their unfitness for the 'sorge weorces' (for there is no hint in the Old English poem that Adam and Eve were put into Eden to work),[13] and their lack of protection and shelter, they appear now to consider the fallen state in Paradise as itself a punishment, although Adam still considers immediate banishment to hell as a possibility. Tormented by hunger and thirst, and at the mercy of the extremes of frost and heat which attacked the fallen angels in hell (325–6), Adam has no hesitation in laying the blame at Eve's door and concludes,

> 'Swa me nu hreowan maeg
> aefre to aldre thaet ic the minum eagum geseah'
>
> (819–20).

> ('Well may I rue it to all ages
> That ever my eyes had sight of you.')

Eve replies with grief but without blame, and Adam relapses into despair of ever being able to work the will of God again. They separate, seek the covering of the forest, clothe themselves with leaves, and unite in prayers every morning. The fragment ends with simplicity, and even with some finality:

> 'ac hie on gebed feollon bu tu aetsomne
> morgena gehwilce, baedon mihtigne
> thaet hie ne forgeate god almihtig,
> and him gwisade waldend se goda,
> hu hie on tham leohte forth libban sceolden'
>
> (847–51).

('Both together they bowed in prayer,
Each morning beseeching Almighty God
That He would not forget them, that the gracious Lord
Would teach them how to live thenceforth in the light.')

*   *   *

How does this poem stand in relation to developed story and
personal myth? Whilst it in modern terms gains some advantages
from its fragmentary state—it is unlikely, for instance, that its
striking opening with the prohibition was to be its real opening,
and no doubt the final scene of reconciliation and prayer
represents the end of an episode rather than of the whole plan—
it seems to me clear that the poet wrote with a forceful artistic
conception and a distinct view of the Fall in mind, and that
these are closely connected. The arrangement whereby the two
Falls are juxtaposed is related to the parallel between God as
lord and Satan as would-be lord, and the use of the messenger is
related both to this and to the emphasis on deception, which, as
we have seen, gives rise to a comment on the scheme of things
which is more lyrical than a moral or doctrine. Moreover, the
use of heroic terms, the broad parallel between heroic society as
seen generally in heroic poetry (whether or not it existed in
reality) and the halls of God and Satan with their respective
retainers, remains generalised even as it is artistically well interwoven; it can hardly be said that there is here an adverse
comment on the system or even that the Satanic society notably
differs from that in heaven except in the essential given fact that
one is run by Satan and the other by God. The poem, in fact,
relies on established attitudes and beliefs, whether or not it was
written in part as an evangelistic document for a pagan society.
The poet's view is backwards to authority or authorities—this
is not the story of a mutiny in a Germanic army and Adam and
Eve are not a typical couple from near contemporary society
who happen to re-enact the myth. If disobedience to their Lord,
like that of Satan, is fraught with the associations of society as it

appears in Germanic and Old English heroic poetry that is because it was the only way in which they could be seen, but primarily these are the first man and woman of the scriptural account.

The themes of deception and of the lord and his thegns have penetrated deep into the fabric of what we have, but, as it were, simply so, in a free and relaxed manner. There is no staggering message, perhaps no notion, even, that the biblical story is a confused one which needs to be straightened out and brought up to date if its 'real' import is to be made clear. There is enough of the heroic system in the relatively plodding *Genesis A* to suggest that the conceptions of the later poem are common ones, produced by the accretion of many narrations of the same story-pattern. The form of *Genesis B* may indeed have derived from the intrigue of deception and disguise rather than having been generated by a traditional form and order of events, but, however that may be, the result as we have it is a unified whole, a distinctive version of the myth rather than a personal version produced independently or deliberately as parallel or contrast.

4. *The Faerie Queene*, Book I

'My mother calls the Fall a mystery; redemption is so too'
—Abel in A. H. Clough, *The Mystery of the Fall.*

The first Book of *The Faerie Queene* is not ostensibly concerned mainly with the Fall. It is rather part of a larger vision of the education of perfect knights in a perfectible England. But it is also a unified whole standing apart from the other books both in its form and as a highly individual version of the Fall myth. I say 'highly individual' because the poem is curiously modern in its structure and its methods, particularly its handling of 'point of view'—that is, a dramatic regard for who at any moment may be speaking. Yet it is also retrospective, both immediately in that its physical world of woods and meadows, as its elaborate and varying scales of virtues and variety of bogies, has, even for Spenser's day, an old world flavour, and in that it employs as background (and finally as foreground) a biblical frame of reference. It is perfectly true that the props from *Genesis* and *Revelation* in the later cantos do not play a part here in a direct retelling of biblical stories for themselves, but equally they are 'lifted' from the biblical sources for the poet's purpose of a re-telling of the myth, and their implications depend on our recalling their original settings, depend, that is, on substantial orthodoxy.

On balance, it seems that Spenser is more interested in re-telling the Fall and recounting the morals derived from that story and its sequels, than he is in portraying his own myth which happens to parallel the biblical and dogmatic versions. This is not so true of the whole poem as it is of this first Book. I think this is partly demonstrated by the fact that the Red Cross Knight does not conclude his earthly quest and the poem never reaches the predicted conclusion; the knights do not attain perfection and the feast (in which each was to recount his story) does not take place at Elizabeth's court. But this, as has already been said, is a matter of degree. Spenser has certainly moved a long way from the Old English poem, and his consciousness of the typicality of the Fall myth, its repeated relevance, does in part take him away from a filling in and updating of the biblical account. It is the fortunes of the Red Cross Knight that he tells; the Red Cross Knight is some sort of Adam, who falls from a qualified paradise, while Una's father, in the 'argument' of Spenser's letter to Raleigh but 'an ancient King', in the poem is the first Adam fallen from, or besieged in, an Eden through which flow 'Phison and Euphrates' of *Genesis*. Una has a queen as mother, but she does not play the part of Eve and indeed the original Fall is not recounted here. Thus the version is at once in the past, in the present of Elizabethan prospects, and out of time as well, for Spenser's treatment is a very eclectic one.

*   *   *

When in the *Letter to Raleigh* Spenser refers to an 'allegory, or darke conceit', he touches on a matter which Raleigh himself had written about, whether or not Spenser had read him or knew he was concerned with it. Allegory, for Raleigh, is indeed a dark conceit. His consideration of it in connection with the *Genesis* story shows that he regarded it as so dark that it was liable to have no meaning at all. He rejects the notion that 'Moses's description of Eden was altogether mystical and allegorical, as Origen, Philo, Georgius, with others, have affirmed'. He dislikes St Ambrose 'who also leaned wholly on the allegorical construction, and set paradise in the third heaven, and in the virtues of the mind'. With the commentators he tries to ascertain the site of an historical garden, and he brings forward the number of translations regarding Paradise as a literal situation 'as proof of this place, and that this story of mankind was not allegorical'. He seems to see allegory as opposed to historical fact, or at least a danger that it may be opposed. He mentions approvingly that Augustine in *The City of God* sets forth three attitudes to Paradise and three classes of people who hold them—'the one of those men which will have it altogether corporal; a second of those which conceived it altogether spiritual, the third of those who take it in both senses,' and he seems to dispose himself firmly in the first class, 'and yet I do not exclude the allegorical sense of the scripture; for as well in this there were many figures of Christ, as in all the Old Testament throughout'.[1]

The Faerie Queene is very deeply concerned with the Fall myth, but not always overtly so, and more concerned with the Fall as a recurring fact of life than as an historical event. From this we cannot conclude that Spenser did not accept it as an historical event, yet certainly we cannot decide that Spenser shares Raleigh's apparent aversion, despite its qualification about the 'figures of Christ', to an allegorical reading. In fact, I think we must say that, wherever Raleigh really belongs, Spenser falls squarely into the third category that Augustine gives. He offers numerous classical versions of the Fall, although, in Book I, he seems to think that the Christian version surpasses them in truthfulness. He sets his whole poem in a general context of historical degeneration (see the Prologue to Book V), with which he associates disguise and deception as well as an inversion of true values, though this context was widely current, being influenced by the Four Ages of Ovid's *Metamorphoses* and possibly by the exposition of the subject in Renaissance commentaries on *Genesis*.[2] He had in fact a vast bulk of material, Classical and Christian, before him which dealt with the Fall, and he chose to place the Christian Fall, historical and recurrent, to the fore. Certainly Spenser did not shrink from the 'allegorical', both in Raleigh's sense and in wider senses, and he can hardly, from the evidence of the poem, have regarded it as an undesirable contradiction to the real or the historical. Moreover, leaving the 'third heaven' aside, he does seem to see some sort of paradise in 'the virtues of the mind'.

In his *Hymne of Heavenly Love*, Spenser seems to view a historical Fall as a partial explanation for that recurrent fall of which the Red Cross Knight becomes, in Book I of *The Faerie Queene*, an example. The *Hymne* relates in the time-honoured sequence the creation of the angels, their fall, the creation of man to replace the lost angels, and the Fall of man, though a few Platonic ideas are mingled with the mainly orthodox doctrine of the poem. In several respects this short version of the Fall is close to Milton's. The motivation of the angels in their rebellion is pride, and they are led by Lucifer:

> 'But pride impatient of long resting peace
> Did puff them up with greedy bold ambition,
> That they gan cast their state how to increase
> Above the fortune of their first condition,
> And sit in God's own seat without commission;
> The brightest Angell, even the Child of Light,
> Drew millions more against their God to fight'
>   (78–84).

Man was created to fill the 'waste and emptie place' left by the banishment of the angels, created of 'clay, base, vile, and next to nought', yet made in God's own image and 'according to heavenly pattern'. The human Fall is taken for granted so far as detail is concerned, though it in unspecified ways parallels the Fall of the Angels:

> 'But man forgetful of his makers grace,
> No less than Angels, whom he did ensew,
> Fell from the hope of promist heavenly place,
> In the mouth of death to sinners dew,
> And all his off-spring into thraldome threw'
>   (120–4).

Spenser goes on to recount the Redemption of man by Christ as man—for

'In flesh at first the guilt committed was,
Therefore in flesh it must be satisfyde;
Nor spirit, nor Angell, though they man surpas,
Could make amends to God for mans misguyde,
But onely man himselfe, who selfe did slyde'

(141-5).

—and to suggest the type of the good life which this sacrifice
enjoins.

This is of course a travesty of the poem, whose orthodoxy and
relation to Spenser's own work have been much disputed.[3] But
what concerns us is first the evident assumption of Original Sin in
some sense—the Fall, or whatever it represents, had a lasting
influence on the human situation—and second the contrast of
the poem's artistic approach with the methods of *The Faerie
Queene*. The *Hymne* may or may not also be an allegory or dark
conceit, in some of Raleigh's senses, but it is primarily a chronological account, prefaced, concluded, and interspersed with
meditations, certainly, but single in its narrative, and on the
whole simple and direct in its exhortation. Whether or not it is a
very good poem, it seems clearly a poem of complete certainty.
What it omits—such as the whole story of the nature and motivation of the Fall of Man—it can afford to omit, because
evidently it can take it all for granted in the reader's mind.

*   *   *

In both method and subject *The Faerie Queene* is a far more complex and even a more speculative work than this; yet there is no
strong reason to suppose that, in the mind of such a comprehensive thinker, with such a habit of assimilating and including,
they are contradictory rather than complementary.

As is characteristic of works concerned with the human viewpoint on the Fall, Book I is composed of sections or blocks rather
than a straight and single narrative. One function of this arrange-

ment is no doubt that of introducing suspense. While it may be true that we never consider the adventures of the Red Cross Knight and Una to be incapable of a happy ending (whilst indeed it comes as a surprise that they do not have in the poem a finally simple happy ending) the form of alternating tales cannot but appeal to us above the optimistic conventions of romance to arouse in us doubt and interest as to the next instalment. The method is to break up one narrative and intersperse it with another, and this has effects more important than the simple one of sustaining interest. Not only may one narrative significantly parallel or contrast with another, as we have seen in the Old English fragment and *Paradise Lost*, but the connection between the blocks, or lack of connection, may be of a thematic nature which is better suggested than imperfectly stated and oversimplified. Not that the links are left out. For Spenser the reverse is true; generally very full links are made— but they are only in complex and doubtful ways accurate assessments of what has happened.

The precise temporal sequence of events in *Genesis B* is open to doubt, and on that doubt hang the questions of why humanity was created, for what reason Satan rebelled, and how far evil is an invincible and eternal force. On it hang also the tone and governing interests of the poem—for man, though he was not created first, appears first in that part of *Genesis B* which we have, and presumably therefore had always a high priority in the poem's interest. It is significant that our vision of Hell and Satanic schemes precedes and governs our vision of Eden, but it is still more significant that we have seen God and man before we have learned of Satan. We do not know how Satan knew of man's existence or of the prohibition, but the obscurity here is not necessarily the result of literary incompetence. In fact it does not press itself on our awareness, nor would it have been difficult to construct a plausible fiction to explain these things. Such a fiction would, on the simplest viewing, have clarified the allegory, but of course it could deny essential elements in the myth, or the allegory in the deepest sense.

There are points in Spenser's poem also which are not 'dark conceits' merely because we have lost some of the keys (though doubtless many have been lost) and cannot go right in, but because the deepest aspects of the poem, however moral its intentions, can only be seen through a glass darkly, and it has succeeded if it can show us this. Some of the obscurity is inherent in the structure. First there are the three sections of the overall narrative, the first ending in the separation of Una and the Red Cross Knight, the second in the rescue of the Red Cross Knight by Arthur, and the third with the climactic vision at the end of the poem. The middle section is composed of alternating narratives. Although this plan for the middle section tells us what was happening to each character at the same time more nearly than would the method of completing one tale before starting the other, the work as a whole is so constructed as to contradict such temporal scrupulousness, and the sequence of events, so far as we can trace it, is very far from being the sequence of events as, in a simple sense, it occurred.

Spenser—like the Old English poet and Milton—starts 'in the middle of things', and, again, it is not merely a matter of grasping the reader's interest by opening with a bang. It is true that Una and The Red Cross Knight are the immediate subject, and that this method of starting highlights the fact whilst it also ensures that we realise that their story is but one episode in a longer series of events. But the more important consideration is that, whilst the notion of sequential time had yet to be questioned by the Age of Relativity, and the notion of cause and effect is certainly vital to the poem, that causal conception of time does not apply to the religious sphere, or not absolutely so. Eden was lost not in the distant past solely, but is being continually lost and found, as the 'original' sin is being perpetually re-enacted or resisted. It seems partly to suggest this that the menaced Eden is not described at the start of the poem, where logically it belongs, but in the middle (Canto VII). The historicity of a first fall is neither affirmed nor denied in any exclusive terms, and the state of the Red Cross Knight at the beginning is neither totally depraved nor totally paradisaic; Adam is not only the first man, but all men, of whom the Knight is one. So there is in the very form of the Book that same struggle between the eternal and changeless God of Sabbaoth and the Titaness Mutability (who is for Spenser firmly attractive rather than odiously seductive or false) which is worked out in the fragmentary *Mutabilitie Cantos*. To place before the story of Una and the Red Cross Knight that of an earlier Fall would be to imply a severe limitation of the free will to resist, and it would also suggest more importance in the historical role of events than, perhaps, the poet is prepared to assert.

*   *   *

There is another apparent obscurity in Spenser's method which we must consider before looking more closely at Una and the Red Cross Knight. Apart from the usual distinction between 'moral' and 'historical' levels of allegory in the work, there are other levels on which the poem moves. On one level it is a series of adventures of heroes, characters not very rounded, but in themselves individual enough, opposed by representatives of evil forces, a story indeed of goodies and baddies, except that the baddies are always more extreme than the goodies. The scene certainly varies, whether it is England, or Ireland, or Faeryland, or just another part of the forest, but it is on this level conceived topographically, although the country cannot be mapped, and its events adhere to a loose temporal sequence. But on another level it is a country of the mind, and the events do not occur chronologically, but are as it were *sub specie aeternitatis*. The two levels coexist. The order of one is loosely temporal, but that of the other varies, being at times of some spiritual development, at others corresponding to stages of liturgical ritual, at others apparently governed mainly by the literary demands of intensi-fication or relaxation; and sometimes, maybe, there is no very essential order at all. On this second level the characters met with are aspects of an implied mind which happen to be dominant at a particular time. They are not necessarily absent at other times, but they do not then require the literary focus to be set upon them. Thus the Red Cross Knight, meeting Pride, is looking at himself in a mirror at this moment. The work depends on this conception, although it cannot be more than implicit; always we are in the odd position of supposing that we know more than the hero, and yet we never quite know what it is that we know;[4] frequently it is not so much that he does not recognise his enemy because of a disguise so much as that, even when he does recognise him, he does not realise until very late in the book that what he meets is a reflection of himself. Yet again the thing is complicated; for these giants and abstractions blend in with each other, their edges and their definitions are not clear-cut. Thus we have the odd situation that the Red Cross Knight, who we are repeatedly told suffers from Pride, yet twice meets Pride, in different forms, and fights a battle with it. He does not win; but, supposing he had done so, would he have gone away any the less proud?

We have to be wary of the idea of a great psyche composed of all the characters in the poem. I think it is real enough, but it has to be kept distinct from that peculiarly modern sense of solipsism, of an all-inclusive mind lost for want of external reference, which threatens to break into discussion of it. There is certainly an important way in which the first part of the Book is lacking in direction and purpose, in which the mind is un-balanced and the ship, in Spenser's recurring image, has no clear course. But the elements of this mind are not entirely dependent on their relationship with other elements for their existence. It is not mainly a relativistic conception, any more than is the handling of time. God is undoubtedly outside this mind, and Alma, the soul, Reason, and self-knowledge, should certainly be in control of it.

Consider the situation at the outset. The Red Cross Knight has illustrated his own pride, and Spenser's comments have drawn attention to it (although it is no single or simple flaw) before he enters the House of Lucifera or is confronted by

Orgoglio. Whether this pride is common to humankind or is of an exceptional degree, the reader is left to decide for himself. At least Una is without it and warns him of his tendency to rash self-confidence, and he replies:

> 'Ah Ladie (said he) shame were to revoke
> The forward footing for an hidden shade;
> Vertue gives her selfe light, through darkness for to wade'
> (I, 12).

We recall the words of the Elder Brother in Milton's *Comus*, words which may or may not appear justified by the course of events, and of one who observes that:

> 'Where an equal poise of hope and fear
> Does arbitrate th'event, my nature is
> That I encline to hope, rather then fear . . .
> (*Comus* 410–2).

> 'He that has light within his own cleer brest
> May sit i'th center, and enjoy bright day,
> But he that hides a dark soul, and foul thoughts
> Benighted walks under the mid-day sun;
> Himself is his own dungeon'
> (381–4).

The Elder Brother's antithesis is too clear to fit the circumstances. It is not evident that the Second Brother harbours a dark soul and foul thoughts, nor is it certain that the Lady herself fits on one side or the other of his distinction. Una makes no such division, and the Red Cross Knight does not fit it, but he is shortly to be in a situation related to that of the Lady in *Comus*, and he is approaching it 'full of fire and greedy hardiment' (I. 14); Una's caution cannot be turned aside with the observation 'how charming is divine philosophy' (*Comus*, 476). It is not idle observation or an over-epigrammatic judgement; we perceive that 'sudden mischief' may indeed 'rash provoke' the Red Cross Knight as he is depicted here. Una, in the poem, is a voice to be listened to 'straight'; but in the assessments of the poet-speaker, as we shall see, there is no such clarity.

Lucifera and Orgoglio, as Una's cautions indicate, are features of the mind always present in some degree, but suddenly striking it in horrendous embodiment when concurring with 'sudden mischief'. It is a question whether the fact of the appearance of these figures is not equally important as anything they may, on the active level, do to the Knight. In Lucifera's palace he is not totally overwhelmed by Pride. He dislikes the house's inmates and estranges himself 'from their joyaunce vain'. Yet this contempt is itself not necessarily an unqualified virtue and the fact that he visited the house in the first place has to be related to the many earlier references to his pride, and, however mildly, laid against him, for the stated reasons for his visit are perfunctorily ludicrous—that Duessa led him (which was his fault) 'for she is wearie of the toilsome way', and it was getting dark (IV, 3). That he is led by Duessa follows as some sort of consequence of his first fall.

In his other encounter with an embodiment of Pride he is felled by Orgoglio, but not killed by him. In fact he is rescued by Duessa. The story must certainly go on and it cannot do so if the Red Cross Knight is killed—there is this crude reason for his rescue. But what exactly is the difference between being overcome by Pride and killed by Pride? His rout at this stage is virtually total. He has been having a rest and had unwisely doffed the Pauline armour. Moreover, as in his dream early in the poem, 'the eye of reason was with rage yblent' and he 'burnt with gealous fire' to see

> 'Where that false couple were full closely ment
> In wanton lust and lewd embarrassment',

so here he has not only taken off the protective armour but also

> 'Goodly court he made still to his Dame,
> Pourd out in loosnesse on the grassy ground'
>   (VII 7).

Clearly Pride as here conceived is no simple thing but a complex of flaws and states of mind.

This is an instance of how, after the first (so it appears) experience of sexual feeling in the dream in Canto I, the Red Cross Knight may employ himself when his confidence gets the upper hand, and the arrival of Orgoglio, a monster of false assurance verging paradoxically on despair, is a proclamation of the fact. He cannot of course enjoy his rest and simultaneously fight for his life with Orgoglio, but evidently the fight with Orgoglio is, seen in one way, less an advancement of the narrative than a symbolic representation of some mental struggle which accompanies the Knight's complacent lying about. But how can that pride, for which he is to be blamed, be opposed to some other pride, which seems to advance on him from outside, and how can they fight together when each apparently represents the other? One will not get far, I think, by trying to list the types of pride or defining their distinguishing features.

Yet the difficulty here cannot be called a confusion or an inconsistency in a pejorative way. Dark conceit it may be, and historically especially so, but there was probably never a key which would produce a set scheme of nicely defined merits and deficiencies. There is great advantage, whatever the superficial awkwardness, in an allegorical method which externalises and yet leaves uncertain the full extent to which things are external. The poet is partly portraying a sequence of events with a moral meaning dependent on a process of education and experience. Nothing should lead us to depreciate the authenticity of this level of action. But he is portraying also a mind at war with itself, divided at this stage among its members, and it is the peculiar power of his mixed allegory to suggest this. In Book II he goes on to develop an ironical level. For Sir Guyon is, in the first part of the Book, above all a man whose mind is ostensibly under control and properly ordered; and yet the second part of the Book reveals that this control is rigid and exclusive to such an extent as to be seriously inadequate.

Thus, in the relating of 'internal' and 'external' events in *The Faerie Queene* there is a radical ambiguity as to how far allegory, as a simple equivalence of meanings, is going. It is all too easy to resolve all difficulties by resorting to paradox, but I think that we may find in this uncertainty a profitable confusion which is one reason for the poem's range and inclusiveness. We do not, despite the most strenuous efforts, infallibly know what originates in our own minds and what enters from outside. It is a problem central to the issue of the origin of, and culpability for, evil, and Spenser, whose poem is superficially so unrealistic, is realistic in the extreme in the way he repeatedly raises it.

*   *   *

As has been noted, this uncertainty occurs, in versions of the Fall, particularly in the dream which Eve may have before her actual temptation, and here it is worth considering more closely the parallel scene in *Paradise Lost*. The significance of the dream is two-fold. First, it is of course a warning: Eve should not have eaten the fruit anyway, but, having had the 'troublesome dream' (in which she did not certainly eat the fruit but thought that she gained some of the enlarged vision it could bestow— *Paradise Lost*, V, 64ff), she should have been doubly resistant to the temptation. Forewarned is forearmed. Secondly, this dream is of obscure origin. On one level it is simply given to Eve by Satan, who appears in it as an angel (for the dream represents the temptation by the angelic messenger which appears in the Old English poem and its traditions), 'one shap't and wing'd like one of those from Heaven by us oft seen' (V, 55), but is in fact

> 'Squat like a toad, close at the ear of Eve;
> Assaying by his Devilish art to reach

> The organs of her Fancie, and with them forge
> Illusions as he list, Fantasms and Dreams'
>> (IV, 800–3).

But on another level it can only occur because evil is in some way already present in her mind, and this Adam tries to explain:

> 'Yet evil whence? in thee can harbour none,
> Created pure. But know that in the Soule
> Are many lesser Faculties that serve
> Reason as chief; among these Fansie next
> Her office holds . . .'
>> (V, 99–102).

Then Adam, consoling Eve for her dream, and trying to assess its implications for himself as well, goes on to state a doctrine entirely orthodox but which later events cause us to call in question, although it is not to be supposed that Milton doubted the doctrine:

> 'Evil into the mind of God or Man
> May come or go, so unapproved, and leave
> No spot or blame behind; Which gives me hope
> That what in sleep thou didst abhor to dream,
> Waking thou never wilt consent to do'
>> (V, 117–21).

This is the version of the dream which on the whole we are to accept—that it was a warning to Eve which she in fact did not sufficiently heed; it was God's way of helping her, in His generosity, to do what she should have been able to do by herself. But Adam's account of the origin of the dream is not in every respect in accord with this view and neither is his conclusion entirely in accordance with the facts of the case. For actually Eve did not clearly 'abhor to dream' despite her 'damp horror' (65). She felt rather that her will was rendered powerless and she 'could not but taste' (86). If she did abhor, it was only for the space of one line, and in all probability the abhorrence was in part a back-reading of the waking mind. But for Adam the dream included 'evil' which was mercifully 'unapproved'. The difference between 'approving' and 'not abhorring' appears marginal. The argument is that 'it was all a dream anyway and has no bearing on conscious living', and yet, at the same time, he asserts by the word 'abhor' that moral discrimination was after all still in force during the dream. Though the doctrinal position may be as Adam states, we are yet faced with the contradiction that it is a good thing that the evil was 'unapproved', and it is also a good thing that it was only a dream. Eve is exceedingly fearful of this unvoluntary passing of evil through her mind. Adam, after initial bewilderment, at least affects not to care a jot. Yet his reasoning appears not without an element of the charm of 'divine philosophy'. The reader sympathises with the notion that evil passing through a mind is nonetheless evil and frightening, and he sympathises also with the distinction which Adam offers as a practical solution—what occurs in dream does not of necessity occur again in real life.

There is in Milton's picture here the same blurring of the edges as we have noted in *The Faerie Queene*; the evil dream is and is not evil, depending on whether or not it is confirmed by the will. It is caused by the direct intervention of Satan as an outside agent, yet his activity concurs with something already present in the mind. Eve has not fallen by having the dream, and yet I think we feel, and Milton felt, that the dream goes beyond the generosity of a warning and hints at the inexplicability of evil and its origins even as a version of the Fall is attempting to clarify these matters.

The doctrine which Adam offers had already been offered by, among others, St Augustine, who, in a series of passages, himself discusses the problem of how external evil can ever have had any effect except by coinciding with potential evil in the mind of the victim;

'But evil began with them secretly at first, to draw them
into open disobedience afterwards. For there would have
been no evil work, but there was an evil will before it; and
what could begin this evil will but pride, that is "the beginning of all sin"? . . . . This evil therefore, that is, this
transgression, was not done but by such as were evil before
. . . So that the devil could not have seduced mankind to
such a palpable transgression of God's express charge, had
not evil will and self-love got place in them before . . .'[5]

Eve in her dream is deceived, though she is reassured by
Adam. When it comes to actually eating the fruit, Adam himself is 'not deceav'd' by the serpent but 'fondly overcome by
female charm', though as to whether this is a worse deception
we are left to draw our own conclusions (IX, 998–9). In the
Old English poem the emphasis on deception (by disguise) is,
as we have seen, uncommonly weighty, and this seems to be
associated with similar ideas on the obscurity of the origin of
evil.

The Red Cross Knight is also deceived by disguise, and
moreover he is so deceived by a dream. Is it the case here
(I, 47—II, 6) that evil may come and go in his mind 'so un-
approv'd' and leave no spot of blame behind?[6] Eve, for St
Augustine and for Milton's Adam, may live unfallen in Paradise
and have evil thoughts, whether of self-love or pride, passing
through her mind, for they are not significantly evil till they are
confirmed by an act of will, and it is axiomatic to these writers
that the will, despite the evil presence, is entirely free. Are we to
suppose that the Red Cross Knight, worked upon in a dream by
evil spirits summoned by Archimago, and moved to such an
extent that he can be called 'bathed in wanton bliss and wicked
joy' (I, 47), is no less unfallen than Eve, and no less free? I
think in theory that we are. But we are again, as in Milton's
handling of free will, placed in a position where there is the
highest tension between our conflicting allegiances. The evil is
there, so to speak, before it appears or is confirmed, as Pride is

there before Orgoglio arrives or before the Knight enters the House of Lucifera. It may be that the yielding to deception is not itself a sin, and it may be that the deception takes place when it is useless to say that all the rational powers should have been deployed to resist it. Again, it may well be that the poet strictly observes the view that evil crossing the mind does not control the mind. But it is certain that both he and the reader feel the full force of the opposite opinion. He leaves us in no doubt that here is a crux of the first order and that, though this is not the First Fall, it is nonetheless a comparable moment from which subsequent misfortunes arise.

Despite the stress on lust in the lines, the Fall of the Red Cross Knight is not a matter of succumbing to lust, but of succumbing to deception and acting on it, although, as we have seen, lust, pride, and the propensity to be deceived, are regarded as associated. It is hardly before he takes his rest with Duessa (Canto VII) and makes 'goodly court' to her that sexual feelings in reality overcome him, but of course the fact that the deceptions with which Archimago assaults him are erotic is not without significance, for the Knight appears as sexually innocent, aware of erotic power yet afraid of it. The separation of him and Una, as critical to events as is Milton's separation of Adam and Eve, will come about partly because of the consciousness of his own purity and annoyance at Una's apparent impurity. Jealousy is an assertion of the value of fidelity even if, unawares, the Red Cross Knight becomes supremely unfaithful by departing from Una at first dawn. It is an assertion of fidelity to himself, for jealousy and fidelity appear here to be related as opposites just as are Pride and self-respect. Even before his Fall the Red Cross Knight is singleminded and even obsessive in his determination to prove a worthy knight, to a degree we perhaps do not much consider until we are invited to make a comparison between a true and a false St George as Archimago disguises himself to be a Red Cross Knight; then, when we make the judgment that the enchanter falls short of the dress he dons, so we also consider how far the Red Cross Knight himself measures up to the role

Archimago is trying to imitate. And then we feel that, though it is not impossible for Spenser to idealise and aggrandise knighthood in a way which we are now perhaps over-ready to read ironically, that opening description of the Red Cross Knight does contain within it a certain overloading, an excessive and exclusive self-reliance and determination, which is the germ of a criticism of the Knight:

> 'Upon a great adventure he was bond,
> That greatest Gloriana to him gave,
> That greatest Glorious Queene of Faerie lond,
> To winne him worship, and her grace to have,
> Which of all earthly things he most did crave;
> And ever as he rode, his heart did earne
> To prove his puissance in battell brave
> Upon his foe, and his new force to learne,
> Upon his foe, a Dragon horrible and stearne'
>
> (I, 13).

But, though indeed the Red Cross Knight's fall is due to deception, being deceived is not in itself sinful, even though preceded by a state of mind potentially evil. This state of mind Spenser has sufficiently suggested by the fulsomely sexual temptations and the anxiety of the Knight (his 'wonted fear of doing aught amiss'—I, 49), who does not in fact fall for a sexual temptation directly. The state of mind has to combine—as Una has said—with 'mischief', with a particular set of circumstances, before, issuing in a voluntary act, it constitutes a fall—such at least seems to be the theoretical position. The Red Cross Knight, though for a while he believes Una to be a 'loose leman' as a result of his dream, has not taken the step. He still can 'temper' his 'fierce despight' with 'sufferance wise'. He is entirely within Archimago's power, in that he can be totally deceived by a dream, yet, if deception is all that can be gained, Archimago's 'labour all was vaine' and his spirits have spent 'bootelesse

paines', although, of course, without that deception, he could go
no further.

What, ironically, the Knight does respond to is not Una sen-
sually disguised as such, but the second delusion of Una apparently loving a young squire. Moreover, it is not merely the
difference in the temptation which issues in a decisive action by
the Red Cross Knight, but the additional fact that he, who
throughout the Book tries to take necessary rest, has had a dis-
turbed night. He is off duty, as a Christian Knight can never be,
and at last taking 'more sound repast', when he is violently
interrupted by Archimago and half-upbraided for having a good
sleep—

> 'Rise, rise unhappy swaine,
> That here wex old in sleepe, whiles wicked wights
> Have knit themselves in Venus shamefull chaine'
>
> (II, 4).

Now he responds with action; the 'sufferance wise' which tem-
pered an impulse to slay the wanton Una of his dream, gives
way to an eye 'with rage yblent' and it is Archimago who restrains, rather as Iago initially restrains Othello when he too is
blinded with jealous rage. The 'gealous fire' of injured honour,
the ready belief that Una is now acquiescing in what he himself
had dreamed of, persists after the sleepless night so that he without
further question commits the decisive act and flees from her.

In this it is Spenser's triumph to have presented an action
which, coolly analysed, can fit a pattern of orthodox doctrine,
but which, read straight through, is surely indefinite and shattering as well as realistic. We recognise where the bounds of
good and evil theoretically lie, between the two dreams, but we
see that in practice they shade into each other and the warning
dream exerts an impalpable influence on the action from which
it is supposedly divorced.

*   *   *

The nature and significance of the Red Cross Knight's Fall and subsequent education are governed by the setting, which in effect defines him as a typical being outside history—an Everyman—and at the same time a man with a special destiny within history—a St George. Although the false Una of Archimago's making has informed us that the Knight's 'own deare sake forst me at first to leave My Father's kingdome', and although we may have read the *Letter to Raleigh*, it is not until the middle of the book that we learn the background to the adventures of the Knight and his Lady. That background is the loss of Eden, with three of its rivers, an event uncertainly related to the story of Adam and Eve. Principally, we are no doubt to understand that Paradise, however lost, can be regained. Those who have failed to defeat the dragon (who originates in *Revelation* XII, where he is identified with the 'old serpent' of the Fall and the chronological confusions begin) have done so 'for want of faith or guilt of sin'—we need not press for a decision between the two to apply to the Red Cross Knight (VII, 45). It can only be regained if it has first been lost, and that paradox, that fallen life is the prelude to redemption, to a state arguably preferable even to the unfallen state, is latent throughout the poem, as it is throughout *Paradise Lost*. We are not told how this Paradise was lost, though it is now menaced by the Dragon, and we may or may not assume the historical priority of the Fall of Adam and Eve. In the poem, however, as it is laid out before us, we enter here upon the timeless level on which the last Cantos move, and the fall of the Red Cross Knight in the poem precedes the menaced Eden. It is going too far to say that this Fall is a duplicate of that of Adam, but the arrangement is such that we perceive a strong analogy between the two. As the Red Cross Knight's spiritual education, though it is a prelude to sainthood in this instance, exemplifies the 'narrow way' which all follow to redemption, so his fall is a version of the ever-recurring sin of Adam. We have seen that there is in the Knight, as in Augustine's example, an 'evil will' or 'pride' preceding his fall, but of course the Knight's fall, the recurrent fall, is in this respect less problematic, for he falls from

a state in some degree already fallen, from a qualified sort of
Eden. Though his tale must parallel that of Adam and Eve, it
cannot be an exact copy, for he is a Briton of historic ancestry
(X, 65-6), neither Adam himself, nor yet a representative from
the world of Faery, whose occupants can neither fall nor be
redeemed.

For the Faery, despite the wondrousness of its supernatural
power which Spenser is at no pains to minimise, has not the
potentialities of the human. It is in the paradoxes of the 'middle
state of man' that the Red Cross Knight is instructed in the
House of Holiness, where the climax is a reminder to him that,
despite appearances, he is not rightly to be 'accompted Elfin's
sonne', but is 'sprong out of English race'—to which he replies
with reassurance and relief:

> 'Thou hast my name and nation red aright,
> And taught the way that does to heaven bound'
>
> (X, 67).

This limitation of the Faery race stems from its origin in
another version of the Fall, which Spenser recounts in Book II
(X, 70ff). This is the story of Prometheus, the only begetter of
the sprites, who, for stealing fire from heaven in an attempt to
animate his created man, was cast out and irretrievably condemned; from his creation sprang the faeries. Prometheus is not
included in Book I, but Spenser gives the related tale of Aesculapius, whose aid Duessa invokes to heal Sansjoy and who again
was considered by Jupiter to have usurped divine powers (this
time in the medicinal field) and was struck by a thunderbolt.
More particularly in Spenser's version he is condemned in
chains to a hellish cave 'deep, darke, uneasie, dolefull, comfort-
less' for reassembling the corpse of Hippolytus.

Both these legends, in Spenser's versions, are of a fall akin to
that of the angels, motivated by hubris on the part of the aspirer.
They represent what may seem a reasonable claim on behalf of
humanity which is punished absolutely and without prospect of

mercy. As such, of course, they contrast with any Christian Fall (save for the theme of aspiration to spiritual knowledge which plays no part in Spenser's version), and indeed the code of simple revenge which they follow is common to the three pagan Sarazzin brothers and is epitomised here (V, 26) by Night in her consideration of the 'sonnes of Day':

> 'Yet shall they not escape so freely all;
> For some shall pay the price of others guilt;
> And he the man that made Sansfoy to fall,
> Shall with his own blood price that he hath spilt'.

But, if they have no vital part in the myth of the Fall as it occurs here, they are nonetheless important in the poem's scheme. For towards this group of ideas—inflexible justice, fate, pride, revenge, hopeless guilt—the Red Cross Knight inescapably moves. He, fallen as it were in the Christian rather than the Classical manner, fallen by a voluntary act of infidelity rather than by a more simple hubristic aspiration, yet moves in his mind towards the Classical total damnation, and thereby he approaches the ultimate infidelity in the Christian scheme of things—the state of total spiritual Despair. Here again close distinctions may be made—perhaps they must be made—but the poet has embodied the complexity of things in his suggesting rather than stating the middle way between the just and the unjust senses of guilt.

The Red Cross Knight's recognition of his guilt seems to mark at first the end of a tension between the reader and the poet, or between our conception of the Knight, and his own. Here at first seems to be realised by the Knight himself that judgement which we passed on him as he deserted Una and, retrospectively, on him even unfallen at the start of the poem. But it turns out that this recognition by the Red Cross Knight is but the reverse side of his previous pride and assurance (inseparable as these are from the desperation of his self-control), and he is no more able to see himself clearly than he was at the outset. Here again allegory is in part an externalisation of a state of mind—a state of mind very understandably following on the crisis with Orgoglio and the rescue by Arthur.

The speeches of Despair are not spoken by the Red Cross Knight—yet they might have been. They have a recognisable affinity with the soliloquies of Dr Faustus in despair. Pride and Despair are met by the Knight, but also they *are* the Knight when he meets them:

> 'Thou wretched man, of death hast greatest need;
> If in true ballance thou wilt weigh thy state . . .
> Is not enough, that to this Ladie milde
> Thou falsed hast thy faith with perjurie . . .
> Is not he just, that all this doth behold
> From highest heaven, and beares an equall eye?
> Shall he thy sins up in his knowledge fold
> And guiltie be of thine impietie?
> Is not his law, Let every sinner die;
> Die shall all flesh? what then must needs be donne,
> Is it not better to doe willingly . . .'
>
> (X, 45–7).

From this state the Red Cross Knight is rescued by Una. She announces the doctrine of Grace and the Knight is rescued from Despair by her, rescued also by allegory, for the inner change of mind which denotes this rescue is not dramatically depicted. Faustus, on the other hand, is alone and of himself is not capable of accepting the doctrine. For Faustus death is feared as the gateway to an eternity of torment, whilst for the Red Cross Knight it temporarily appears an easy oblivion. Faustus's mind is opened before us as the Knight's is not, and it is not possible for him to express convincingly the distinction between penitence and the sense of guilt which cannot logically be explained to the unbeliever:

> 'What art thou Faustus but a man condemned to die?

Thy fatall time doth drawe to finall ende,
Dispaire doth drive distrust unto my thoughts,
Confounde these passions with a quiet sleepe;
Tush, Christ did call the thiefe upon the Crosse,
Then rest thou Faustus quiet in conceit . . .
Where art thou Faustus? wretch what hast thou done?
Damnd art thou Faustus, damnd, dispaire and die'

(1143–8, 1285–6).

The tension is the same. We see that faith, which goes with penitence, is so easy a thing and yet so difficult, that Faustus at one moment has it, or a semblance of it (when Mephisto observes 'His faith is great, I cannot touch his soul'), yet is repeatedly defeated by a physical fear which to us, detached, is irrelevant. The Red Cross Knight, again on the verges of penitence and despair, has a similar delusion, for the concept of total death which he welcomes is as irrelevant as are Faustus's tortures. Both men, one terrified out of faith by physical fear, the other tempted from it by illusion of physical and mental peace for evermore, are at critical moments and in the event one will fall further and the other rise up.

It is in the House of Holiness that the Knight, after his rescue by Una, comes to recognise true repentance as distinct in quality from an overpowering sense of guilt, though the difference is indeed so narrow that Una finds 'herselfe assayld with great perplexitie' when he 'greev'd with remembrance of his wicked wayes . . . desirde to end his wreched dayes'. But once again allegory can suggest without explaining and it is again a merit of the method that it can give us both sides of the issue and leave us to face it.

*   *   *

As of penitence, so of all values in the poem—we cannot find them simply and acceptably defined, though simple definitions which are only partially acceptable are many. When we bear in mind the stanza quoted on the Red Cross Knight's aspirations to 'winne him worship' (I, 3), how far can we view Spenser, at least in the first Book, as a straightforward commentator directing our judgement, and how far as a calculated persona whose stated view may lie a subtly judged distance from the apparently intended view, from the view which makes sense, if of the part, of the part within the context of the whole? How much twentieth-century love of ambiguity and complexity are we importing when we speak of it as being ironic (apart, of course, from dramatic irony where an event or remark anticipates another)?

I think it is fair to say that Spenser is more often ambiguous than ironic;[7] he frequently gives the comment of one character on another, without indicating how much of the assessment is his (or the writer's, for we are not interested in autobiography) own, but there is an unmistakable detachment in the openings of his cantos where the writer purports to speak directly to the reader. This matter is clearly of importance in determining one area of the poem's success or failure; if the poet can be ironic, it follows that certain clumsinesses, omissions, or obscurities (barring such a lacuna as what eventually happened at the end of Canto VI, which seems to have been simply overlooked) may well be deliberate, or, if that is not an acceptable term, may be regarded as genuine and integral rather than as breakdowns in artistry.

We can consider as a relatively simple example the opening of Canto III, and as a far more complex case the opening of Canto V. No doubt the author's persona has good reason to be sorry for Una, but we may doubt the adequacy of the comment which starts Canto III in an almost Chaucerian manner:

> 'Nought is there under heavens wide hollownesses
> That moves more deare compassion of mind,
> Then beautie brought t'unworthy wretchednesse
> Through envies snares or fortunes freakes unkind;
> I, whether lately through her brightnesse blind,
> Or through allegeaunce and fast fealtie,

Which I do owe unto all woman kind,
Feele my heart perst with so great agonie
When such I see, that all for pittie I could die'.

'Such' can refer to the poem's situation, in which case the reaction is exaggerated or unreal, or to parallel events in real life, in which case, though we do not doubt the sympathetic mind, we qualify the response by the patness of the final couplet and the vast and indisputable generality of the opening. Spenser's love for Una is a very constant feature of his comments, but that does not make it any less ironic. We are aware that Una is viewed as admirable, and we know that an artist can fall in love with a character he has created, but this love, stated baldly and openly, is more metaphorical than real. Spenser's direct address to his characters, so far from reinforcing the dramatic element in his poem, its total 'embodiment' and 'realisation' of a typical situation, is a violation of the totally dramatic or novelistic as we know it, not dissimilar to the comments of Smollett or Sterne upon the lovable inanities of a wandering hero. It is not that we are to ignore such intrusions, but that they are not entirely and simply applicable to the situations before us. The poet is a character in the poem, but the effect is not to make the poem a total and self-contained dramatisation subject to peculiar laws of its own.

There is, I think, a narrow and important distinction here. Just as, in the presentation of the elements of one mind, we are not left with the sense of that mind existing self-sustained, but with the idea that, properly ordered, it is related to Reason and God, so the poet's detachment, his refusal to make a certain 'moral', relies on the assumption of secured values in the light of which we qualify his comments. There are, certainly, occasions, when if he has pointed to a heart of mystery, that is all the 'moral' there is or need be, but the commoner method where the characters of the poem are concerned, is to provide comment which by its inadequacy and our sense of its inadequacy allows us to test our own reading, our own values. No one, presumably, supposes that Spenser's 'fraile eyes these lines with teares do steepe' is to be taken literally when he considers Una's 'divorce' from her Knight, but it is more than the melancholy pose of an inferior sonnetteer poured forth by rote; it is an image of sympathy with Una and judgement of the Red Cross Knight which courteously indicates the way our reactions may go but does not order us to adopt any defined position.

From Spenser's way with the relatively simple case of Una we infer a similar method for handling attitudes to the Knight himself. The telling phrases ('ficklenesse', 'rash misweening', 'lightnesse and inconstancie in love', 'light misdeeming of her loialtie' (IV, 1–2)) have no single effect upon us. Our response appears rather to be three-fold; first we accept them as a solid judgement of the Red Cross Knight, a fair assessment of his case; then we reflect that that case is more complex than any to which such judgements might fairly be applied; finally, we place again the case and the judgements alongside each other and perceive that after all from a certain point of view they fit closely. That viewpoint is of course the one of severe justice, the viewpoint which the Knight himself takes when he is nearly overcome by Despair, and which both he and the reader come before the end of the poem to balance with a view of mercy—mercy as a mystery which, like Grace or the arrival of Arthur, may or may not occur, depending on things beyond our understanding.

We therefore accept the comments as examples not of the poet's incompetence but of his realisation that he is dealing with matters ultimately inexplicable. For example, the following passage is clearly not an adequate summary of the import of the action. It does not answer our questions and it does not entirely accord with what we have seen. We grant that 'heavenly grace' has rescued the Knight, but not with the same moral pacifism and inevitability as the words imply—for Spenser's use of Grace does not, when viewed in context, make the Knight's predestination to sainthood beyond doubt and there is free will as well as determinism at work in the poem. We grant indeed that the Knight fell in some sense through 'foolish pride or weaknesse', and that he is 'upheld' by Grace, but neither so in an unqualified manner:

> 'Ay me, how many perils doe enfold
> The righteous man to make him daily fall?
> Were not that heavenly grace doth him uphold,
> And stedfast truth acquite him out of all.
> Her love is firme, her care continuall,
> So oft as he through his own foolish pride,
> Or weaknesse is to sinfull bands made thrall . . .'

It is all true—Una remains faithful to the Knight, Arthur supports Una in crisis; but it is also oversimple.

Whether we call this use of categorical judgements which do not quite fit, 'ironic' or 'detached' or 'complex', it seems clear that they are in intricate relation to the context. We are startled by the opening of Canto V, where the Red Cross Knight plans how best to fight Sansjoy, and how to emerge 'with greatest honour', terms which in themselves refer back to earlier references to the element of ambiguous pride within him:

> 'The noble hart, that harbours vertuous thought,
> And is with child of glorious great intent,
> Can never rest, untill it forth have brought
> Th'eternall brood of glorie excellent;
> Such restless passion did all night torment
> The flaming corage of that Faery knight . . .'

We are invited to ponder whether the Red Cross Knight now has a 'noble hart that harbours vertuous thought' when he is intent on winning glory in a battle he should never have had to fight, when the 'flaming corage' is presented in the ludicrous light of a mother about to give birth. We go through the usual process of deciding that this is really how the rather inconsistent poet regards him, then deciding that it is approximately the reverse of how he views him and is a form of contemptuous belittlement, and finally concluding that even a Pyrrhic victory is better than a defeat and the terms have some relevance to the hero after all, only that they are appropriate to his unawareness of his own limitations. The ambiguity continues when we are informed that he 'not a pin does care for looke of living creatures eye' (V, 4), that 'all for prayse and honour he did fight', and that 'th'one for wrong, the other strives for right'. The 'rights' are the shield of Sansjoy, which is really no concern of his, and fidelity to his lady of the moment, the false Duessa, whom he will soon worship as his 'Soveraine Queene' (16) and who is bent on doing all the harm she can.

*   *   *

> 'What man so wise, what earthly wit so ware,
> As to descry the crafty cunning traine
> By which deceipt doth maske in visour faire,
> To seeme like Truth, whose shape she well can faine,
> And fitting gestures to her purpose frame,
> The guiltlesse man with guile to entertain?'
>
> (VII, 1).

What man indeed? Evidently not the Red Cross Knight, and the possibility has further to be reckoned with that none at all can reliably see so far. Here, as it were, is a comment on the comments, a further invitation not to respond too readily to appearances. It escapes no reader that one of Spenser's major themes is deceit and disguise, that he presses for as close a relation between opposites, disguised as each other, as he can achieve. Yet he leaves us with the impression that this susceptibility to deceit is peculiarly the characteristic of the fallen world, as it is the property of the fallen to fall more easily further. Arthur accepts it as the human condition:

> 'But th'only good, that growes of passed feare,
> Is to be wise and ware of like agein . . .

This dayes ensample hath this lesson deare
Deepe written in my heart with yron pen,
That bliss may not abide in state of mortall men'

(VIII, 44).

Pride and deceit, like pride and jealousy, are closely linked. Pride is a deceit of the self. When the Red Cross Knight, who hath ever but slenderly known himself, meets Lucifera, he meets the embodiment of this connection, aptly named after the arch-proud deceiver Lucifer. As we have seen, the fall of the Red Cross Knight is only in a special way due to Pride, and it is a way less clear than in cases like those of Prometheus or Aesculapius. But, for all the subtlety of the portrayal of his mind, reinforced by the uncertain viewpoint of the poet's speaking persona, Spenser leaves us in little doubt that pride is in some way involved centrally, and that Pride takes more than one form. Lucifera and Orgoglio as types of Pride overlap, but they are also in some ways distinct.

The episode with Lucifera and her palace is prefaced by the poet's remarks on the Knight's 'ficklenesse', 'rash misweening' and 'lightnesse and inconstancie in love'. Some of these descriptions are shortly also given to Lechery (who is 'false and fraught with ficklenesse' and is an 'inconstant man') leaving us in no doubt that the Knight's indulgence with Duessa, his exclusive self-reliance, and his mistrust of Una, are all interconnected. His deception is at once limited and total; he does not know that he has been deceived about Una, but he is aware of his infidelity, holding it fully justified by the circumstances. It is a pardonable error—for in another context this same determination would be praiseworthy—but it is not pardoned. It is caused by the deception of Archimago, but that deception was in part the outcome of the Knight's own self-delusion.

It is, therefore, entirely fitting that, after his defeat of Sansfoy to gain as prize the apparently rich booty of Duessa for his pleasure, and after his total blindness to the close resemblance between the situations of Fradubio and himself, the Red Cross

Knight, confident and victorious, with the so inadequate 'sleeping spark of native virtue' revived, should meet the embodiment of Pride which, though real enough, is founded on ignorance of self:

> 'It was a goodly heape for to behould,
> And spak the praises of the workmans wit;
> But ful great pittie, that so fair a mould
> Did on so weake foundation ever sit;
> For on a sandie hill, that still did flit
> And fall away, it mounted was full hie,
> That every breath of heaven shaked it;
> And all the hinder parts, that few could spie,
> Were ruinous and old, but painted cunningly'
>
>   (IV, 5).

The description of Lucifera and her shoddy palace is a supreme instance of a dialogue between nature and art (misconstrued), truth and falsehood, which runs through the poem.[8] Lucifera, the female Lucifer, is compared with Phaethon, another case of hubris,

> 'That did presume his fathers firie wayne
> And flaming mouthes of steedes unwonted wilde
> Through highest heaven with weaker hand to rayne'
>
>   (9).

and who, although penitent, was cast headlong by Jupiter's thunderbolt. Her pride is clearly that of a false self-regard:

> 'And in her hand she held a mirrhour bright,
> Wherein her face she often vewed fayne,
> And in her self-lov'd semblaunce took delight'.

The daughter of Pluto and Proserpine, she, like Phaethon, disputed her parentage and claimed 'thundring Jove' as her father. She 'seemd as fresh as Flora in her prime' (17), and we recall that Archimago's false Una was crowned with an ivy garland by 'freshest Flora' (I, 48). As we have seen, it is typically ironic that as the Knight left Una in the conviction of his own righteousness (but, for us, in a mood of dangerous instability and impulsiveness), so now he will not accompany Duessa and Lucifera, with her company of Idleness, Gluttony, Lechery, Avarice, Envy, and Wrath. In his fallen state, he cannot make a choice which is wholly right. We perceive the merits of steering clear of this crew of Deadly Sins, but we perceive also a certain snobbish pride in the refusal:

> 'But that good knight would not so nigh repaire,
> Himselfe estraunging from their joyaunce vaine,
> Whose fellowship seemd far unfit for warlike swaine'
>
> (37).

'Unfit' the 'fellowship' doubtless is or should be, but it is not easy to tell how much of that epithet 'good' and of that description of a 'warlike swaine' is the poet's and how much the knight's own estimate of his status. Yet again, the opposite assessment, offered by Sansjoy ('this recreant knight/No knight but treachour full of false despight/And shamefull treason' (41)), is felt to be excessive condemnation. As throughout the first part of the Book, and throughout the rest of the poem as a whole, the concern is with the middle state of fallen man, so here, and repeatedly, it is the 'middle way' which, it seems to be implied, we should take in our judgement of the Red Cross Knight.

The account of Orgoglio is also preceded by stanzas suggestive of a point of view which very much complicates what appears at first sight a simple enough pattern of moral extremes. First there is the statement (quoted above) of the near impossibility of going through life with 'earthly wit' undeceived. Then there are the stanzas on the Knight's dalliance with Duessa, his first real experience, it seems, of the 'great passion of unwonted lust' which awoke him from his dream of the false Una in the first Canto. We have not seen him since he escaped from the palace on being told of the horrors of Lucifera's dungeons by the dwarf at the end of Canto V. Moreover, we have been given a false sense of equanimity by the innocence of the intervening canto, where Sir Satyrane rescues Una from Sansloy (the canto terminating rather abruptly with a loose end). Art and the moral pattern are united in this interweaving of tales, for the pastoral interlude gives to the reader some of the assurance and some of the respite which the Red Cross Knight now supposes himself to possess. The reader has taken off his armour as well and is unprepared for a second, and more deadly, assault of Pride.

Again the descriptions have their ironic element, but not so ironic as to amount to actual inversion—'the noble Redcrosse knight', 'this gentle knight', 'goodly court'. The Knight, understandably deceived by the false Una and then more culpably taken in by Duessa, now deceived by the need for rest and the 'pleasaunce of the joyous shade', is then still more excusably deceived by the fountain which drugs him and takes away his 'manly forces'. It is an ignorance of information directly imparted to the reader and for which the reader consequently hesitates to blame him, but it is a misunderstanding with disastrous results.

Whether the doped fountain released in him an evil hitherto latent in his mind, or whether he is suddenly overcome by something new to his experience, we cannot well decide; but clearly this technical trick of revealing to the reader what the victim could, in ignorance, hardly understand, may symbolise the impotence of the mind confronted by certain situations. It is an externalisation of something felt to be inherently inexplicable, irresistible yet evil and making the patient culpable. We have the sensation both that the Knight could not help himself, and that he is guilty of a wrong moral choice—a recurrent dilemma in the poem.

In the description of the giant Orgoglio who stalks into the scene of pastoral repose the emphasis is less on his self-deceit (though he is 'puft up with emptie wind' and, like others we have seen, 'great with arrogant delight' of a false ancestry) and more upon the terror he causes. With his weapons untimely disposed around him, the Knight is saved from the first blow, though knocked over by its wind, by 'heavenly grace' and not by any virtue of his own—he who is made faint by the power of the fountain and is 'disarm'd, disgrast, and inwardly dismayde' (that is, 'in pieces'). Conserved by Duessa for a state of eternal slavery worse than death, the Red Cross Knight mentally disintegrates; the coexistence of pride and weakness, of assurance and self-deception, of purity and goodly court, are too great a strain and rescue can only be from without.

*　　*　　*

Although it is preceded by the passage already noted as requiring qualification (on the 'perils' which threaten every 'righteous man' and which can only be met by 'heavenly grace'), the arrival of Arthur marks a turning point in the poem, not only in the action, but in the nature of the poetry; hereafter it is less dramatic and less uncertain, rather lyrical and ritualistic, working towards the few certainties which will make sense of the previous complexities and the Knight's dismembered personality. It is the one large-scale moralisation, but, outside the opening passage, even this is not directly thrust at the reader, despite the fact that the distinction between poet and Spenser—that is, the sense of irony and detachment—gradually lessens.

Here also, the level of the action begins to change; in one sense it broadens to take in a world above human, and in another it narrows to give due stress to the Knight's intended historical role. Hitherto, despite the reference to St George in Canto II (12) we have been concerned with an Everyman who will not recognise himself as Everyman. He is a fallen man who understandably falls further to the depths of abasement, until Arthur intervenes and he gradually progresses by hard lessons towards self-knowledge and sainthood. I say 'hard lessons', because it seems to me that the 'education' must be viewed in this way—the supernatural power of Archimago, and the special circumstances which coincide with the Knight's individual character and its potential weaknesses, are directly opposed by the supernatural power of Grace and Arthur its representative which coincide with the character's potential strengths; but how far success is due to the learner's efforts on the one hand, or to those of the teachers on the other, must remain obscure. We have already noticed the paradox by which the Knight cannot achieve the state of sainthood until he is fully aware of himself as a man 'sprong out of English race, However now accompted Elfins sonne' (and however called an 'Elfin knight'), and that, in the end, he has still a term of earthly service to carry out. The last part of the Book is to be concerned with the education and penitence of fallen man, but also with the elevation of the Red Cross Knight to an exceptional goal and an exceptional symbolic act overcoming the dragon of present discontent and showing the possibility of defeating the original Serpent. The Knight's extremes of self-praise and self-condemnation were accompanied by the ironic poet, and, with the victory of Despair with the help of Una, both disappear.

The episode with Despair seems to be another attack of the malady glimpsed in the struggle with Orgoglio, and, as that struggle was preceded by the Satyrane interlude and the Palace of Lucifera before that, so here again, before this ultimate depth, there occurred the lighter-hearted section in which Arthur told of his love for Queen Gloriana-Elizabeth, and exchanged gifts with the Red Cross Knight. In the confrontation with Despair we, and the Knight himself, are at last offered a true and unexaggerated account of his misdoings. We are moving out of the world of deceitful and disguised appearances into a world where the facts are clear and where it is their larger context which counts for everything; this is the perspective in the light of which the previous assessments were corrected by the reader. Thus the two questions of Despair (IX, 46–7) are each presented in the same matter-of-fact, indisputable fashion, and it is with something of a shock that we realise that they are contrasted and we are having to change our position and the grounds of our sympathy with the Knight. He is no longer represented as the victim of sleight-of-hand deceptions and we are to recognise a certain kinship with him. Whatever the causes and the extenuating circumstances, the human consequences are the same, and the only hope is in seeing them in the context of a different law from that of retribution and absolute justice which has most frequently appeared hitherto:

> 'Is not enough, that to this Ladie milde
> Thou falsed hast thy faith with periurie,
> And sold thyself to serve Duessa vilde,
> With whom in all abuse thou hast thy selfe defilde?
>
> Is not he just, that all this doth behold
> From highest heaven, and beares an equall eye?
> Shall he thy sins up in his knowledge fold,
> And guiltie be of thine impietie?
> Is not his law, Let every sinner die . . .?'

The Red Cross Knight, 'knowing all true', has no answer to it. Una puts forward the doctrine which alone, in the poem, can make sense of an all-or-nothing situation where there is either total guilt and total punishment or total innocence and pardon:

> 'In heavenly mercies hast thou then no part?
> Why shouldst thou then despeire, that chosen art?
> Where justice grows, there grows eke greater grace,
> The which doth quench the brond of hellish smart . . .'
>
> (IX, 53).

The opening of the following Canto (X) exemplifies the new status of introductory comments—

'What man is he that boasts of fleshly might,
And vain assurance of mortality,
Which all too soone, as it doth come to fight,
Against spirituall foes, yeelds by and by,
Or from the field most cowardly doth fly?
Ne let the man ascribe it to his skill,
That thorough grace hath gained victory.
If any strength we have, it is to ill,
But all the good is Gods, both power and eke will.'

We may indeed not accept the doctrine of grace, or we may qualify the very low estimate of human capability which the stanza seems to put forward—though it is low, and the role of grace special, because the Red Cross Knight's case is special, and the fact that he is 'chosen' need not argue a general acceptance of a doctrine of predestination. [9] But, whether we accept or reject them, we can see that this is a distinction made in all seriousness between the weakness of man and the felt strength of divine power, that the apparent exaggeration here, if we still sense one, springs from the moving of the poem towards a more lyrical level, where it is ultimates and the largest of generalisations that are being considered. There may certainly be argument in the sense of persuasion or emphasis, but it is argument from premises which are firmly established and assumed to be so by the poet.

The question with which the Canto opens is virtually rhetorical; it is not expected that any sensitive reader will deny that all, or virtually all, mortals will lose a spiritual battle which they try to fight without the aid of grace or the intervention of Arthur. There is a certainty of fundamental assumptions here that there is not in any previous part of the poem except those parts concerned with Una and the poet's love for, or faith in, her. It is here that the Red Cross Knight is brought into line with these assurances and, at the House of Holiness, acquires a balance of knowledge of and repentance for his guilt. The close association of despair, pride, and sin is still apparent, and his first reaction to hearing from Coelia 'of God, of grace, of justice, of free will', is one of despair, from which Hope and Patience rescue him, but after which a penance of almost medieval mortification is still necessary to cure 'the cause and root of all his ill/Inward corruption and infected sin' (25–8). Only then, succoured by Charity and Mercy, is the Red Cross Knight fit to experience the vision of the New Jerusalem which sets his earthly quest, Gloriana (Elizabeth), and the city of Cleopolis (London), in the larger perspective which they lacked in the first part of the poem.

Once again, it is a balanced acceptance rather than an exclusive rejection of the worldly which is favoured:

'Till now, said then the knight, I weened well,
That great Cleopolis, where I have beene,
In which that fairest Faerie Queene doth dwell,
The fairest city was, that might be seen . . .
But now by proof all otherwise I weene;
For this great Citie that does far surpass
And this bright Angels tower quite dims that towre of glass'

(58).

The Holy City is not described at length. It is not a triumph of artifice such as Lucifera's palace, which can be set forth in virtuoso detail, but something which can best be suggested (with echoes from the Bible, Jacob's vision of angels ascending and descending and the fuller description of the Heavenly City in *Revelation* xxi–ii):

'Of perle and precious stone, that earthly tong
Cannot describe, nor wit of man can tell;
Too high a ditty for my simple song'

(X, 55).

But Contemplation—at last the innocent version of the venerable old man who keeps popping up disguised and evil earlier in the poem—will not readily allow the reality of Cleopolis to be

rejected out of wonderment at the Holy City, any more than
Arthur or Una or Speranza would permit the Knight to abandon
his earthly life for a presumed higher purpose or because of his
recognition of his own sinfulness:

> 'Most trew, then said the holy aged man;
> Yet is Cleopolis for earthly frame
> The fairest peece that eye beholden can;
> And well beseemes all knights of noble name
> That covet in th'immortal booke of fame
> To be eternised, that same to haunt . . .'
>
> (X, 59).

Spenser may be harping on the ancient debate between the
active and the contemplative life and opting for the former. But,
equally, he is opting for the fallen state as the only gateway to
the unfallen:

> 'O let me not (quoth he) then turn againe
> Backe to the world, whose joys so fruitlesse are;
> But let me here for aye in peace remaine,
> Or straight way on that last long voyage fare,
> That nothing may my present hope empare.
> That may not be (said he) . . .'
>
> (63).

*   *   *

With the vision of the New Jerusalem we enter upon the last
section of the poem, more purely lyrical and symbolic than anything before. Here much is done by suggestion and analogy
rather than by plain or argued comparison; 'so darke are
earthly things compard to things divine', but the divine things
are less amenable to earthly language and processes of thought.
The Knight is reinstating the Eden desecrated by the dragon—
Spenser is pointing at once to a future triumph over all evil, to

an end of the fallen state, to the historical freedom of England from Spain or Catholicism, and to the individual expiation and atonement of the Red Cross Knight for his particular fall. Thus it is an event on both planes of the poem, temporal and timeless. We remember it, perhaps, principally as the eternal symbolic victory, but, on the temporal level, it does not of course end the poem, and there remain the years of earthly service which the Knight has to perform for Gloriana (XII, 18).

There can be no hard and fast distinction between these levels; it is profitless to argue that, because six years of service are specified, this can have no reference to the return of the fallen state, or that the victory over the dragon does not in some sense resemble a total and future victory over all sin. It had always been so, for the War in Heaven in *Revelation* was both the source for versions of the Fall of the Angels which followed it, and a vision of the ultimate triumph of God. In these last Cantos all levels meet, with comprehensiveness and suggestiveness, if inevitably with no rigid logical consistency.

Gradually in the eleventh Canto the biblical and religious imagery grows more dense. We cannot tell whether the 'living well' which alone could terminate Fradubio's imprisonment (II, 43) strictly anticipates the 'well of life' into which the Red Cross Knight fortunately tumbles, and which flowed with medicinal powers (like the English Bath and the German Spau!) before the dragon 'got that happy land', but there seems to be a connection between the two. In this well the Red Cross Knight's hands are 'baptised' and he now acquires supernatural strength which hitherto has seemed only to operate against him. In Eden are the 'tree of Life, the crime of our first fathers fall' (46) and the Tree of Knowledge, 'That tree through one man's fault hath doen us all to dy'. From the Tree of Life flows a stream of healing balm, into which the Knight again by good fortune falls.[10]

These are hints, rather than clear-cut versions of a story. It is not clear, and it does not really need to be clear, what relationship between the dragon's attack and the fall of Adam and Eve can strictly be drawn. The poet turns aside to tell us of the grave import of the Tree of Knowledge, but it is not sure how *far* he turns aside—it is assumed within the poem that the original sin preceded the dragon, who now represents the fallen state, or is this a more direct address to the reader at this point? Loosely the dragon seems to represent a lasting menace following on the original fall, yet that he 'all did overthrow' suggests rather that he represents the first catastrophe in general form. What is clear, and what is persistently assumed, is that there is a connection, less than fatalistic but more than coincidental, between the fact that Eden is now so menaced and its king and queen beleaguered, and the minor fall of the Red Cross Knight. Equally, there is no definitive connection, but we feel there is a very strong link, between the Knight's victory over the dragon and a propitiation of his earlier errors on the one hand, and between the victory and his need to return to the fallen world on the other.

Finally, the Knight's quest, whatever the hardship or the failure en route, is traditionally the proving of the man. The Red Cross Knight perhaps looks upon it in this light too rigorously when we first see him, but there remains strongly at the end the paradox that such proof is compounded of defeats, that one must fall before one can rise, that the fallen state may be the way to greater blessedness than there would have been without it. The idea of the 'fortunate fall',[11] though it is not insisted on, is latent throughout the poem.

*   *   *

Spenser's versions of the Fall are numerous and suggestive. He accepts it both as an event in the past which conditions all subsequent action in an inexplicable way, and as an event eternally being repeated. In either case it can be reversed by a combination of action and grace derived from faith. But this is for the individual. His final battle-scene, between St George and the dragon, touches on a more lasting victory in the undefined future, but this is a vision and not a prediction, both on the historical and religious levels.

His peculiar talent for handling the subject is his way of implying but not forcing analogies and connections. In one way the poem is a monument to externalisation, a representation in concrete terms of what goes on in the mind and a representation of a particular instance of what happens in Everyman's life. But in another sense this first Book at least is curiously internal. This is nowhere more evident than in the gradual building up of sequential scenes into a picture of the Red Cross Knight's state of mind, where all the diverse attitudes represent components of one mind before and after the crucial separation from Una, and where, at his nadir, fallen man is full of contradictions related to each other but to no outside certainty.

The poem importantly both employs and recreates the authoritative story—that story is an established context not in doubt. The myth here, at least in outline, is orthodox enough. But there has taken place a considerable change from myth as we see it in the Old English poem, which, despite its dramatisation, is nearer to Spenser's *Hymne* than it is to *The Faerie Queene* Book I. Motive in the Old English poem was a complex matter, but we understood it as such as a result of a skilful process of omission. In *The Faerie Queene* the mystery is included and embodied in the uncertainty as to what happens inside and outside the conscious mind, and what is the relation between these two worlds. The poem is far from gnostic. It is not content to 'set paradise in the third heaven, and in the virtues of the mind'. Yet it evidences introspection accompanying a shift of emphasis in the myth from what is conceived of as having certainly happened in the remote past, to what repeatedly happens in the present, and what, if no way out of the cycle is found, will happen in the future. In its large orthodoxy and retrospection it is developed story, but evidently there is, in the relating of the Adam story to the Red Cross Knight, and in the whole conception of a fallen society by slow education ending up in a heavenly metropolis, much of personal myth.

PART III

The Way of the Personal Myth

5. Romantic Attitudes

'If the power with which wickedness can invest a human
being be thus tremendous, greatly does it behove us to
inquire into its sources and causes'
—Coleridge, *The Friend.*

Something of an adjustment is necessary at this point. It seems
to me clear that *The Faerie Queene*, in its first Book, is a version of
the Fall. It will not imediately be so clear that the works considered from now on are also versions. Therefore I mention again
the position of *Paradise Lost* as both summing up what has gone
before and suggesting some of what is to come. I do not call the
latter 'personal myth' because in any clear way it is known to
represent the personal views of the writer, though to a varying
extent it will doubtless do so, or because it is radically opposed
to another tradition. I think that in fact it is more profitable to
see all versions as springing from the same origins, denying perhaps the unique authority of the biblical story, but assuming
rather that it is itself a part of a still developing myth. Viewed in
this way, aspects of the Old English *Genesis* or *The Faerie
Queene* which are departures from the biblical authority are
nonetheless part of the myth and its development—it is simply
that that development has through the ages accelerated and
Milton's poem represents a notable advance which later versions
continue. We may for convenience class this advance as a change
of kind—as from developed story to personal myth—but really
it is a change in degree and emphasis. That the Romantics start
from an interest in the authority and then find a similar pattern
in other experience from which the authority is virtually
excluded is seen as a further shift in that emphasis. And as they
use other experience as an immediate basis rather than compar-
ing it with the authority—so further developing the 'recurrent'

interpretation already seen—so new themes enter into the central themes of the myth.

The quotation above from Coleridge relates to one of two major interests which Wordsworth and Coleridge found in the Fall. Its context is the repeated discussions between Wordsworth and Coleridge of the theory of Godwin that evil could be explained as always rationally motivated. Wordsworth wrote his play *The Borderers*, containing an apparently motiveless crime, to refute the theory; Coleridge, after hearing Wordsworth read the play, wrote *The Ancient Mariner*, containing also an apparently motiveless 'crime' and also a number of direct allusions to the play, but also introducing the other major Romantic interest in the Fall as being a myth of the state of the specially gifted poet. In this chapter I want to consider first two complete and fairly direct versions of the myth, and then to look more briefly at some other significant and more heavily 'personal' developments.

* * *

Undoubtedly Wordsworth and Coleridge started with philosophical and doctrinal questions related to the biblical story but more particularly concerned with a recurrent Fall. Lamb states that Coleridge intended to write a 'great philosophical poem' on the origin of evil, and Coleridge says that *The Wanderings of Cain* (surviving as a prose fragment) was to be the subject of a poem. Coleridge outlined the scheme; he would write the first canto, Wordsworth would do the second, and whoever finished his assignment earlier would 'set about the third'. The 'exceeding ridiculousness' of these arrangements was almost immediately apparent, and '*The Ancient Mariner* was written instead'[1]—thus contributing to another but never fully executed scheme whereby, of the *Lyrical Ballads*, Coleridge would provide poems of a more supernatural and philosophical nature and Wordsworth 'give the charm of novelty to things of everyday life'.[2]

In the event, *The Ancient Mariner* did not fully support the

Bedford Book of Hours—The expulsion from the walled garden, and the four rivers.

MS Junius XI (Cat. no. 13)—Satan, fettered in Hell, sends the tempter up to Eden, where he coils round the Tree as a serpent and tempts Eve.

Piero della Francesca—St Michael and the Dragon.

Paolo Ucello—St George and the Dragon.

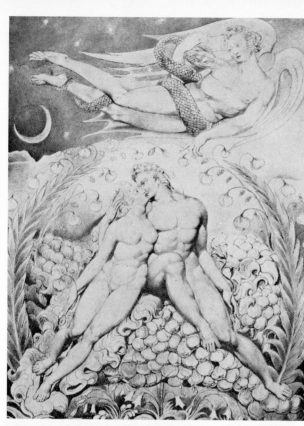

William Blake—Satan
watching the
endearments of Adam
and Eve.

From the film,
Lord of the Flies:
'Having a war or
something?'

theories which Wordsworth set out in his Preface, and, moreover, Wordsworth's 'industry proved so much more successful
and the number of his poems so much greater', especially when
he also included 'two or three poems in the impassioned, lofty
and sustained diction which is characteristic of his genius', that
the effect of the *Lyrical Ballads* and their Preface in the 1798 and
1800 editions was more complex and less clear-cut than originally intended. For our present purposes, however, *Lyrical Ballads*
offers *The Ancient Mariner* and *Tintern Abbey*, which, supple-
mented by *Kubla Khan, Dejection*, and the *Ode on the Intimations of
Immortality*, give considerable insight into the Romantic handling
of the Fall—both as a first or typical sin and in the now emerging conception of the artist in process of creation peculiarly, but
accursedly, able to transcend the normal limits of experience of
fallen man and specially able to recognise those limits.

The immediate prompting of *The Ancient Mariner*'s composition was a dream of the death-ship by Coleridge's friend Cruick-
shank, and to this Coleridge and Wordsworth jointly decided to
add a preceding crime as an explanation of the curse. It was
Wordsworth who decided on the nature of this crime.[3] Whilst
The Borderers amply demonstrated Godwin's notion that nature
takes its revenge in kind on those who offend her, Wordsworth's
insistence that the crime in the play should be as nearly as
possible without motive (to refute Godwin's other theory)
effectively ruined it as a play on this subject. But, Wordsworth
having decided on the nature of the crime and 'the navigation
of the ship by the dead men', and thereby given Coleridge the
outline of a narrative structure (for Coleridge always a problem),
Coleridge was able by his introduction of the marriage guest as
audience to create a work far more profound and also formally
more satisfactory than *The Borderers*. What prompted the device
of the guest we do not know, but it is of course this which adds
the second element of the Fall theme—the status of the poet in
relation to society.

Coleridge borrowed from, or remembered, *The Borderers* more
directly than the mere provision of crime and curse might

suggest. In Act IV of the play Oswald the villain describes to Marmaduke the origin of the evils by which they are beset. We are told how the ship was becalmed under a burning sun until Oswald's fury took control of him and he blamed the captain for their misfortune and determined to kill him. The other members of the 'small troop' which landed on the barren rock to which they had drifted interceded, and Oswald compromised to the extent that they left the captain marooned on the 'bare rock, narrow, and white, and bare':

> 'Naked was the spot
> Methinks I see it now—how in the sun
> Its stony surface glittered like a shield;
> And in that miserable place we left him,
> Alone but for a swarm of minute creatures
> Not one of which could help him while alive,
> Or mourn him dead'.[4]

The burning calm, the need to dig for fresh water, above all, the swarm of minute creatures, which were to become the 'million million slimy things', manifestly impressed themselves deeply on Coleridge's receptive mind and generated the horrors of his poem. To the incredulous Marmaduke Oswald admits that the captain had done nothing against him, 'the man had never wronged me', and here of course is a dramatic weakness; the captain was marooned because 'all hated him', because Oswald in particular was 'stung to madness', and because, in this situation, he was an object on to which the maddening frustration of being becalmed could easily be foisted. It is merely an incident in the play narrated by Oswald; of his state of mind as he tells it we know, but of his state of mind, of the particular motivating conflicts under the head of being 'stung to madness', we know nothing. But when this narrated incident becomes the central subject of a narrative poem, and when the crime becomes, not the killing of a human being in a state of fury, but the killing of a bird whose significance is not known, the mystery becomes a merit. Ignorance will explain why it was wrong to kill the albatross, but it will not explain the impulse to do so. There is no urge to kill the bird comparable with motives for tasting the fruit of the Tree. Coleridge has ensured that his treatment of the Fall shall stress the essential mystery without prejudicing plausibility or literary interest, subject as they are in this case to the qualifications of ballad form, archaic language, and events of long ago.

The actual tale of the Mariner uses symbols which were both well-established in Coleridge's own poetry and also common property in the eastern and occultist thought which exercised an increasing influence on English Literature during and after the later eighteenth century.[5] In Southey's *Inchcape Rock*, for instance (another poem in the popular 'curse' vogue) the Rover steals the bell from the rock as the sun shines. On his subsequent voyage, the sea becomes rough and vengeful; it is foggy, and he hopes in vain that the moon will shine out through the murk to save him from the rock on which he is destroyed; the bell has a warning value which links it with the preservation of human life, and by stealing it he has committed a sin comparable with that of the Ancient Mariner. The sun and moon are central symbols in Coleridge's poem, and they alternate throughout it. Immediately after the bird is shot, 'the sun rose up upon the right'. Initially the sailors praise the mariner's action since, now that the troublesome mist has gone, they imagine that the bird must have caused it:

> 'Twas right, said they, such birds to slay
> That bring the fog and mist.'

But their praise springs from selfishness and ignorance; the mist protected them from the blistering sun to which they are now exposed. Their minds adjust with fickle ease to this new perception and, in unanimous accusation, they lay the dead bird round the Mariner as a token of his 'sin'.

The sun itself is neither beneficent nor malevolent—the

symbolism affects according to the situation of the participants in the action. The moon, if it is usually beneficent, is only potentially so. In Part I, as the bird of good omen appears, and dramatically before the blunt announcement that 'I shot the Albatross',

> 'all the night, through fog smokewhite
> Glimmered the white moonshine.'

But when, in Part III, the seamen all die, the moon rises with a star between its tips and is evidently of reverse significance.

The sailors accommodate their minds to circumstances and justify their behaviour by a rationalism of expediency. By contrast, all the Mariner's actions and thoughts are intuitive. We do not know why he kills the bird, and neither do we know whether, when he looks around at the dead men and thinks it unjust that they should die (whilst the million million slimy things live on), this is a sign of hubris or of a dawning realisation of the principle of life in all things. But there is no doubt that, in Part IV, with the blessing of the snakes, the worship of the 'happy living things', intuitively and 'unawares', we have the turning point in the Mariner's career. Part V, where the moon shines through a gap in the clouds of a violent storm, the Mariner is in a trance, and (from Wordsworth's idea) the ghastly figures of the dead men guide the ship, discusses, by the voices of the Spirits, perhaps representative of the workings of the Mariner's unconscious, the notions of sin and redemption. The first voice laments that he slew the bird and compares this action to the crucifixion (the sailors had hung the Albatross round the Mariner's neck 'Instead of the cross' at the end of Part II). The second says that there is yet hope for him since, significantly, 'his great bright eye up to the moon is cast.' The Mariner awakes from his trance and feels a breeze, which seems related to the wind of the Holy Spirit, and twice it is said that 'on me alone it blew'. The breeze which symbolises (if one may so crudely put it) his redemption intimately connected with his

blessing of 'the happy living things', drives the ship home with
its sole survivor and the load of corpses:

> 'Swiftly, swiftly flew the ship,
> Yet she sailed softly too;
> Sweetly, sweetly blew the breeze—
> On me alone it blew.'

Yet, if this curse is expiated, the man thus guilty and redeemed
is still not unaccursed. For the tale which he tells is under
compulsion. The fact that he tells it and must tell it is an
essential part of the poem, and the tale told occupies only some
two-thirds of the whole work; the setting is as important as the
tale itself.[6] The Mariner waylays a guest at the marriage feast
and the poem is rudely punctuated by 'the sound of the loud
bassoon', perhaps most comical of musical instruments. The
sombre happenings are interrupted by natural social revelry
rather as a contemptuous 'Pok' of the opening of bottles
periodically breaks into any attempt to be serious in Joyce's
Ivy-Day in the Committee Room. The two worlds will not mingle,
and in the end the guest who has been so perfect an audience
turns from the bridegroom's door 'like one that hath been
stunned' and takes no part in the wedding celebrations.

The Mariner presents a weird appearance. His 'glittering eye'
mesmerises and terrifies the guest. The hermit who meets the
Mariner on his return to harbour takes him to be a devil. The
guest says that he appears 'plagued by fiends'. The Mariner is
aware of this effect; he tries to reassure his audience—'fear not,
fear not, thou wedding guest'—and is himself uncertain if the
audience will continue to listen. But the guest reassures him that
he has no choice but to do so, for

> 'That which comes out of thine eye doth make
> My body and soul to be still.'

Even when the guest has endured the tale and the Mariner

makes his desperate appeal for company, the guest, though he will awake 'a sadder and a wiser man', will not accede, and the Mariner is doomed to remain metaphorically what he has been in fact—'alone on a wide wide sea'.

Much has been made of Coleridge's statement that 'the fault was the obtrusion of the moral in a work of such pure imagination'. But Coleridge was always over-anxious to admit to non-existent faults. The 'moral' drawn by the Mariner is a very different thing from the moral effect of the poem. The difference is even greater when the 'moral' is also drawn by the calculated pastiche of the prose gloss added in 1817. We have then a deliberate over-simplification to secure the full effects of distancing and perspective—it becomes a 'tale-within-a-tale-within-a-commentary'.[7] What concerns us more than a 'moral' is more what can be conveyed by Arnold's phrase 'high seriousness'. That this is present in *The Ancient Mariner*, and that it has little to do with the moral 'he prayeth well who loveth well' (by the Mariner) or that he resolves 'to teach by his own example, love and reverence to all things that God made and loveth' (the gloss), seems to me clear. If 'love' is understood in the broadest sense—as, for instance, when Shelley affirms that 'the great secret of morals is love or a going out of our nature'—this may, perhaps, do, but the moral openly obtruded hardly conveys this, for it is the moral still within the poem spoken by a character and a persona. Outside, rather than within, the poem, there is no suitable moral caption but rather a version of the Fall, first as mysterious sin and mysterious redemption, and secondly as the predicament of one who has had supranatural experience and expressed it in words, thereby living under a curse of a different nature.

This secondary curse is to some extent illuminated by *Kubla Khan*. There is no reason to doubt the account of its composition which Coleridge gives,[8] nor that, after it has been examined extensively for the light it throws on his use of memory in composition in general and in this poem in particular,[9] the poem remains obscure and unfinished. But to finish is not necessarily to add to the total bulk; it may be rather to pare and to refine. I subscribe to the view cogently expressed by Humphrey House,[10] that this is a poem whose essential form is settled and meaningful, although the interpretation of every detail cannot be completed because the artist as craftsman has not put on the finishing touches.

Kubla Khan as we have it seems clearly to involve the Fall myth, and to be concerned centrally with that aspect of the myth which the 'setting' of *The Ancient Mariner* suggests—it is a poem about art and the artist in a fallen world. We can say that its form is binary basically, although the two halves are not completely separate and indeed they interact. *The Ancient Mariner* is not purely the narrative poem which it purports to be, but *Kubla Khan* is still less so. The first part describes the pleasure dome which Kubla built, as it were the landscaped garden, the walled paradise, of previous paradises, or the society or personality temporarily at one with itself—not a complete and perfect work of art but a temporary state of balance. The completed work appears rather in the 'dome in air' which it becomes. In the second part Coleridge considers a potential subject for a work of art; either, on Wordsworthian lines, it will be the singing Abyssinian maid as recollected in tranquillity, or, alternatively, the Abyssinian maid serves rather as the nightingale or the skylark or the darkling thrush of other poets who find themselves unable for various reasons to compete with natural paragons of song and yet make mysterious poems of their incapacities. Either way, the division is after the 'caves of ice' on their first appearance; the rest is concerned with the wish to build, and the consequences of building, the 'miracle of rare device'. At the same time, whilst I think this structure is broadly clear, one cannot insist on any detailed interpretation based upon it. An interpretation in terms of art is, I would say, most nearly acceptable, but its real use is in establishing the sorts of conceptions represented by the sections of the poem and their relationship, rather than a reading with which one can agree or disagree.

In the first part of the poem, thus divided, the labyrinthine threads of reading which go to make up the full texture—the threads so expertly traced by Livingston Lowes—are subordinate, from our present point of view, to Coleridge's drawings upon *Paradise Lost* (IV, 214ff). The inverted syntax of the opening

> 'In Xanadu did Kubla Khan
> A stately pleasure-dome decree'

derives, as clearly as it derives from other sources, from Milton's

> 'in this pleasant soile
> His farr more pleasant Garden God ordaind'.

'Many an incense-bearing tree' relates to 'Groves whose rich Trees wept odorous Gumms and Balme'. Milton's 'steep glade' becomes Coleridge's 'romantic chasm'. 'Mount Amara' and 'Mount Abora' seem related. Milton's Eden is 'high raised above a watery current'; Kubla's dome is above a sea into which flows the stream to emerge as a 'mighty fountain' like Milton's 'fresh fountain' which irrigates Eden and then falls back to meet the 'nether Flood' and emerge as the 'four main streams' of *Genesis*. The ambiguity of Coleridge's fountain is parallelled by Milton's fountain; compare the markedly menacing effect when Satan enters Paradise through the fountain:

> 'There was a Place,
> Now not, though Sin, not Time, first wraught the change,
> Where Tigris at the foot of Paradise
> Into a Gulf shot underground, till part
> Rose up a Fountain by the Tree of Life;
> In with the River sunk, and with it rose
> Satan involv'd in rising Mist . . .'
>
> (IX, 69–75).

Kubla's palace is 'with walls and towers engirded round', in the Paradise tradition, and Milton's Paradise is surrounded by a 'verdurous Wall'. Whatever stress we place on individual parallels and other sources, there seems no doubt that in depicting Kubla's pleasure house Coleridge relied on the basic topography of Milton's Eden.[11]

Yet, to whatever extent Milton's Eden was intended to be, or has the effect of, a complete and perfect place, Kubla's dome is a much more precarious affair. Its perfection is rudely shattered by the eruption of the great fountain within and wars prophesied from without. What remains after this destruction is an image:

> 'The shadow of the dome of pleasure
> Floated midway on the waves;
> Where was heard the mingled measure
> From the fountain and the caves.'

It seems to be this image, not the pleasure dome itself but its conception or memory, its 'shadow', complete with sun and ice, which is the 'miracle of rare device', and it is the 'dome in air', not the dome itself, that the poet-figure, however inspired by the Abyssinian maid, would build for himself. The sacred river Alph reinforces this distinction. Coleridge may have recalled Alpheus from *Lycidas*, where Milton employed Alpheus in the dual capacity of unrequited lover, never to meet with Arethusa in the Greek myth, and the poet's unconscious inspiration. Coleridge's 'woman wailing with her demon lover' may be Arethusa, but it seems very clear that Alph represents what we would now term the unconscious, the imaginative pressures and psychological forces which must burst forth in their fountain, even to destroy the pleasures of an established personality or society (the dome itself), to produce (in the 'miracle') the mimetic image of the dome—although in fact the dome itself may be an imitation of the perfect miracle, the ideal work of art and its essence.

If this personality or this society, or both, were so disrupted, and if the image could be made, its creator would bear some

resemblance to the Ancient Mariner and his madly glittering
eye,

> 'And all who heard should see them there,
> And all should cry, Beware! Beware!
> His flashing eyes, his floating hair!'

This is the poet-philosopher of Plato's *Phaedrus*, retaining tran-
sient memories of man in an unfallen state and endeavouring to
impart them to fallen man. It is also to be the outcast poet of the
next 150 years, claiming to have fed on honey-dew and drunk
the milk of Paradise, or at least to offer to an unwilling audience
a unique perception, a new way of seeing things derived in part
from his failure or his refusal to be conditioned by the values of
the world to whom he would speak. He may need to be exorcised
('weave a circle round him thrice'), he would like to be respected
and even revered ('close your eyes with holy dread').

Two points need to be made here. First, *The Ancient Mariner*
and *Kubla Khan* are versions of the Fall which, if they undoubtedly develop the general process of internalisation and the
view of the Fall as ever-recurring, and if they are of small scope,
nonetheless mark a significant development in their closely relating the predicament of the artist to the Fall myth. Whilst of
course Romantic and post-Romantic claims actually to create, to
'repeat the act of the infinite I AM', are many—and whilst the
logical place for the artist in the Fall myth is that of God the
Creator—the main concern with the myth continues to be with
the imperfections of the human lot seen, as it were, from Adam's
point of view. And so a certain confusion creeps in whereby the
artist may be the Creator, or the aspiring Prometheus, or Adam
or the tormented Cain and, in whatever role, he is not only artist
in particular but man in general.

Secondly, although these poems predate (though they may
anticipate and may have contributed to formulating) Coleridge's
most important critical and theoretical writing, our reading of
the poems is conditioned by the critical tradition which he

played so large a part in establishing, a tradition whose central tenet I take to be the 'organic' nature of literature, the impossibility of separating form from content.[12] It may indeed have been because this idea was already growing in his mind that Coleridge remarked on the 'open obtrusion' of the 'moral' in *The Ancient Mariner*; the remark, which seems so inapplicable to a reading of the poem, may have been of a defensive nature, designed to protect him from committing himself to beliefs which he was on the verge of setting out more comprehensively than could be done in an occasional argument.

*   *   *

That Wordsworth was deeply concerned with the origin of evil and the nature of sin has already been stated in connection with *The Borderers*. But this was not in fact to be his main preoccupation so much as was the analysis of his sense of a visionary faculty once possessed, then lost, and finally enlarged. He is not directly concerned with the story of Adam and Eve; indeed, at least by the time of *The Excursion*, he seems to include it as conceivably a 'mere fiction of what never was' (Preface, 1814). Yet Wordsworth, if he could be transiently struck by the insubstantiality of objects touched by his hand, if he possessed momentarily a vision of nature so total and comprehensive as to transcend the need for a Chain of Being or a more ordered system of belief, was of a fundamentalist cast of mind—he did at least think it of importance, as Coleridge did not, whether an Adam and Eve historically existed. His contribution to the Fall myth is of a rather heterodox and oblique nature, but it is nonetheless significant, because the centrality of retrospection in his poetry anticipates subsequent versions of the Fall, whose emphasis continues to swing towards the idea that Adam and Eve, whether or not they existed, symbolise a recurrent situation for individuals.

Tintern Abbey was the penultimate poem in the first edition of *Lyrical Ballads* (and was in fact the last of them to be written), and *The Ancient Mariner* was the first. As has already been said,

The Ancient Mariner conformed with Coleridge's assignment in the joint programme, but *Tintern Abbey* rather differed from what Coleridge had expected Wordsworth to produce (and what in general, for the anthology, he did produce). The similarity and difference between the two poems in respect of the Fall is instructive. Coleridge, of course, concentrates on the supernatural and what may loosely be called the 'theological' aspects, although the device of the narrator points to the personal aspect, whereas Wordsworth personalises and humanises. He—or the speaker—has committed no notable sin comparable with that of the Mariner (however mysterious that may be) but he has been away and he has come back and he is adjusting himself to what he finds. 'Though absent long', he finds that 'sensations sweet, felt in the blood and felt along the heart' have, he now realises, been with him 'mid the towns and cities', have, conceivably, influenced him in a moral direction in 'little nameless unremembered acts/Of kindness and of love', have, more vitally still, from time to time led him on to that deeper and virtually indefinable experience in which 'the heavy and weary weight of all this unintelligible world' (the 'irritable reaching after fact and reason' of Keats)[13] 'is lightened', and 'we see into the life of things.' If this connection be but speculative and a 'vain belief' (for, though the experiences are indubitable, the connections are hypothetical), yet nonetheless the sensations sweet *have* remained. As he stands, the 'sensations' clarify of the time when 'nature to me was all in all' and the difference becomes more certain, the connection less than hypothetical, that there has been a loss and 'abundant recompence' as well:

> 'For I have learned
> To look on nature, not as in the hour
> Of thoughtless youth, but hearing oftentimes
> The still, sad music of humanity.'

This broadening and deepening of what has remained in the mind, at times unconscious, till now not fully realised, this

humanising of what was in the nature of a hedonistic delight, is
one with the 'blessed mood' when we see into the life of things
and now strikes him again as above all comprehensive and
unifying:

> 'a sense sublime
> Of something far more deeply interfused,
> Whose dwelling is the light of setting suns,
> And the round ocean, and the living air,
> And the blue sky, and in the mind of man,
> A motion and spirit than impels
> All thinking things, all objects of all thought,
> And rolls through all things.'

Nor is this process peculiar to himself. He thinks of Dorothy as
much younger than he (though in fact she was only a year
younger) and imagines for her the same development when her

> 'wild extasies shall be matured
> Into a sober pleasure, when thy mind
> Shall be a mansion for all lovely forms.'

Here, then, Wordsworth in effect represents his Preface about
'recollection in tranquillity'. He finds abundant recompense for
what has been lost. In *The Prelude* he outlines a similar notion,
of a first stage when nature was

> 'But secondary to my own pursuits
> And animal activities, and all
> Their trivial pleasures',

an interim state when these

> 'props of my affections were removed
> And yet the building stood, as if sustained
> By its own spirit',

and a third in Book VIII corresponding to the consolatory state in *Tintern Abbey* when love of nature and love of man appear to be inseparably involved. In these statements is a sense of loss but also of consolation—they are the germs of the Fall theme as it is found in Wordsworth.

The consolation proves not to be a lasting one; the visionary faculty atrophies and the definition of the consolation becomes increasingly theoretical. When in 1802[14] Wordsworth wrote the first part of the *Immortality Ode* (as I shall call it), it was a poem of unconsoled loss:

> 'Turn wheresoe'er I may,
> By night or day
> The things which I have seen I now can see no more',

albeit momentarily relieved by the 'timely utterance' of the poem *The Rainbow*, and ending with the unanswerable question

> 'Whither is fled the visionary gleam?
> Where is it now, the glory and the dream?'

The building does not stand, at this moment, as if sustained by its own spirit; its very foundations seem to have gone. In 1806 he looks for consolation in the idea of pre-existence, the soul 'trailing clouds of glory' 'From God, who is our home', but it turns out at best to be explanation rather than consolation. The Youth—the young Hartley Coleridge—is attended 'by the vision splendid' for a while, but

> 'At length the Man perceives it die away,
> And fade into the light of common day.'

Gradually he is conditioned—he falls into the 'frame' of life, 'to dialogues of business, love, or strife'. He plays his various parts on life's stage; society particularly is the difficulty. And, in the end,

'Full soon thy Soul shall have her earthly freight
And custom lie upon thee with a weight
     Heavy as frost, and deep almost as life.'

Clearly this is no consolation, but rather an intensification of the
sense of loss, brought about by projecting his own experience on
to Coleridge's 'six years' darling of a pigmy size.'

Coleridge, having seen the *Immortality Ode* in its first part only,
meanwhile asked himself analogous questions in his *Dejection
Ode*, though his dejection is nearer the state of religious accidia
than the specific loss of visionary experience felt by Wordsworth.
Initially he moves—in a progression we have already seen in
The Faerie Queene—from dejection to despair, where all is seen in
terms of an internal world and all initiative must come from a
spirit incapable of initiative:

'Though I should gaze for ever
On that green light which lingers in the west
I may not hope from outward forms to win
The passion and the life, whose fountains are within.

O Lady! we receive but what we give,
And in our life alone does Nature live . . .
And from the soul itself must there be sent
A sweet and potent voice, of its own birth,
Of all sweet sounds the life and element!'

Coleridge, who criticised Wordsworth for being so attached to
the corporeal world outside himself, for being a 'spectator ab
extra', can clearly in his own different theory of cognition find
no consolation. Yet, as if by a perverse irony, in this poem
addressed to Sarah Hutchinson, where he is all but bogged down
in the despair of the solipsist, he finds a resolution just where
Wordsworth can find none—with the thought of Sarah he
achieves almost unconsciously the magical going out of oneself
and entering into another:

'Tis midnight, but small thoughts have I of sleep;
Full seldom may my friend such vigils keep!
Visit her, gentle sleep, with wings of healing,
And may this storm be but a mountain-birth,
May all the stars hang bright about her dwelling,
Silent as though they watched the sleeping Earth!
      With light heart may she rise,
      Gay fancy, cheerful eyes,
Joy lift her spirit, joy attune her voice . . .'

Wordsworth, by a precisely reversed process, coming back to
his *Ode*, deepening his sense of loss by dwelling on the infant
Hartley, finds his resolution not by a going out but by an entering further in. What he found on revisiting Tintern Abbey was
an enlarging of earlier 'sensations' to a vision capable of containing and not conflicting with the still sad music of humanity,
and that vision depended on a suspension of 'the heavy and
weary weight' of the unintelligible world. Yet now it is for 'those
obstinate questionings' which, as evidence of a supreme mystery
lodged in 'eternal Silence', he raises 'the song of thanks and
praise'. This, I think, is not a consolation, but a stoical acceptance. The glory and the dream are gone, and so is the visionary
gleam which had previously managed to embrace the human
lot. If the lambs bound and the birds sing, 'we in thought will
join your throng'; joining in thought is rather different from an
experience of 'a love'

'That had no need of a remoter charm,
By thought supplied, nor any interest
Unborrowed from the eye',

but it is different too from the survival of those 'sensations' in

'a sense sublime
Of something far more deeply interfused
Whose dwelling is the light of setting suns . . .'

'The thought of past years' may 'breed perpetual benediction', and the more so if the soul which experienced them did so in part because it was born 'trailing clouds of glory', but the conception is an intellectual one, stoically framed to sustain the poet for an indefinite future in serenity yet with a sense of inconsolable loss.

So, a year later, in the *Peele Castle Elegy*,

> 'A power is gone, which nothing can restore;
> A deep distress hath humanised my Soul . . .
> The feeling of my loss will ne'er be old;
> This, which I know, I speak with mind serene.'

Had there not been this loss, he would have been able to paint the Castle not, indeed as it 'truly' or 'really' was as perceived by a high faculty of imagination, but with the *addition* of

> 'the gleam,
> The light that never was, on sea or land,
> The consecration and the Poet's dream,'

—for Wordsworth never subscribed to the 'organic' view mentioned above in connection with Coleridge, though his vision may in practice achieve it.

Wordsworth's versions of the Fall, then, are many but oblique. They are, substantially, accountings for one or other of the lights 'full early lost and fruitlessly deplored'. He is not, after *The Borderers* (and discounting the guilts and fears of *Nutting* and *The Prelude* which are deemed to have an educative value in the humanising of his love), concerned with the problems of sin and guilt, but with the gift of knowledge of a kind peculiarly his own and dependent on solitude. His importance in the Fall tradition is nonetheless almost equal to that of Coleridge, for further directing the myth towards an expression of the situation of the artist as a being typical yet of heightened sensitivity, attuned to the loss of Paradise and seeking to recreate it.

*   *   *

I do not think that, in this respect, either Keats or Shelley is so influential a figure. But Keats in his two *Hyperions* essayed with doubtful success what neither Wordsworth nor Coleridge attempted—a major work specifically on the Fall theme. Our difficulty in assessing them is nonetheless considerable, since Keats's versions are incomplete fragments, dependent for interpretation on much of his other work not directly relevant to the theme.

In *Sleep and Poetry*, which is primarily a poet's dedication to his art, Keats expressed in an intellectual manner something which he was to 'prove upon the pulses' in his grappling with the Fall myth in the two versions of *Hyperion*. Almost from the first, he was

> 'certain of nothing, but of the holiness of the heart's affections and the truth of the imagination. What the imagination seizes as beauty must be truth . . . for I have the same idea of all our passions as of love; they are all in their sublime creative of essential beauty.'[15]

This idea of beauty as truth is a recurrent one, which he progressively defines in the *Odes*, a beauty first sensuous as in *Endymion* and Keats's Spenserian readings; then progressively related to the particularly painful circumstances of his life (and especially the death of his brother Tom, under the shadow of whose illness he attempted to revise the first *Hyperion*), a relation embodied in the 'truth' of the beauteous figures on the Grecian urn (that 'cold Pastoral'), beauty external yet an illumination of rather than found directly in the sufferings of actual life; then achieved, a union in the relaxed perfection of *To Autumn*.[16] In *Sleep and Poetry* Keats dedicates himself to a new poetic ideal, which he calls the 'vast idea' and which he symbolises by Apollo. In company with a host of other poets he will start—has in fact started—with a pastoral phase, 'the realm of Flora and old Pan', the world also of *Endymion* and the *Ode to Psyche* (whom he pledged to celebrate in a solitary and internal temple where 'I will be thy priest and build a fane/In some untrodden region of my mind'). But in time he will surpass these limited interests, seductive as they are:

> 'And can I ever bid these joys farewell?
> Yes, I must pass them for a nobler life,
> Where I may find the agonies, the strife
> Of human hearts.'[17]

These passions will be fused with beauty, for in the purely didactic Keats is not interested. Yet if this fusion is accomplished the moral urge of the poet will also be satisfied. 'Beauty' will not do, and 'Truth' will not do, and only the passions and imagination can unite them. There is danger as great in moral seriousness as in the realm of Flora and Pan:

> 'But strength alone, though of the Muses born,
> Is like a fallen angel; trees uptorn,
> Darkness, and worms, and shrouds, and sepulchres
> Delight it; for it feeds upon the burrs
> And thorns of life; forgetting the great end
> Of poesy, that it should be a friend
> To soothe the cares and lift the thoughts of man. [18]

The first *Hyperion* attempt suggests through the mouth of Oceanus that the Fall of the Titans is to be viewed as part of a cyclical pattern of the replacement of the good by the better:

> 'As heaven and earth are fairer, fairer far
> Than chaos and blank darkness, though once chiefs . . .
> So on our heels a fresh perfection treads,

A power more strong in beauty, born of us
And fated to excel us, as we pass in glory
That old darkness . . . for this the eternal law
That first in beauty must be first in might'
                                        (II, 216ff).

None of the Titans except Oceanus can accept this view. They
are torn between the realisation of their own tragic fall and the
possibility that Hyperion still remains above, but this hope is
dispelled when Hyperion makes his magnificent descent and
completes the fall of the old order. With the exception of the
scene in heaven at the end of Book I, we see everything from the
point of view of the fallen Titans until the unfinished Book III
in which Apollo, the representative of the coming order, is
introduced, passes through an initiation into painful Experience, and then is deified. But of his nature as distinct from that
of Hyperion and the fallen Titans we know nothing, however
we may conjecture from Keats's wide use of Apollo elsewhere
that he represents the ideal of Beauty and Experience fused,
whereas Saturn and the Titans represented Beauty in the innocent and sensuous state.[19] The fall is seen with wistfulness and
resignation, whereas the treatment of the coming Apollo is by
contrast almost frenzied and spasmodic, characterised by the
various abrupt and unsuccessfully attempted conclusions:

'Apollo shriek'd; and lo! from all his limbs
Celestial . . .'

or

'Apollo shrieked—and lo! he was a God,
And godlike . . .'

or, in the most completed version,

'Apollo shrieked—and lo from all his limbs
Celestial Glory dawned; he was a god!'

In the second version, *The Fall of Hyperion, A Dream*, the whole conception is changed. Because of the dream form we now see things not from the point of view of the fallen, but from that of someone else inside the action, and his impression is not of pathos redeemed by faith in a new order (which albeit in the first *Hyperion* did not convincingly emerge), but of an agonised horror at the Fall and lack of consolation for it. The poet is from the first personally involved, guided by Moneta (who replaces the first version's Mnemosyne as the priestess of the old order who will usher in the new). He is accused of being a 'dreamer' and not a poet, and these two are contrasted, not as Keats had contrasted them in *Sleep and Poetry*, but by Moneta, in the following terms:

> 'The poet and the dreamer are distinct,
> Diverse, sheer opposite, antipodes.
> The one pours out a balm upon the World,
> The other vexes it'
>
> (I, 199ff).

The ideal sought in the *Ode on a Grecian Urn*, sought indeed throughout Keats's brief and intense poetic career, was the obliteration of this contrast, and Apollo was to represent the notion of beauty as not separate from but found in, yet also 'soothing', the vexations of human existence.

Hyperion magnificently falls—

> 'His flaming robes streamed out beyond his heels,
> And gave a roar, as if of earthly fire,
> That scared away the meek etherial hours,
> And made their dove-wings tremble. On he flared'
>
> (II, 62ff).

ending the fragment (lines which have far more effect so placed than in the first *Hyperion* I, 214ff). But Apollo never appears, his conception even wilts before the sharp distinction between dreamer and poet which Moneta draws, and we are left with the frustrated

'Apollo! faded! O far flown Apollo!'

Moreover, even the fallen order is not the valued but superseded thing it was to have been in the first version. Now the fallen Saturn simply cannot hear the 'hymns of festival' in the heaven from which he is fallen, nor dream of the 'beautiful things made new for the surprise of the sky-children'. Saturn, though defeated, in the first version uttered his speech and then

'Passion lifted him upon his feet
And made his hands to struggle in the air',

but now he has not even these remains of life in him:

'So feebly he ceased,
With such a poor and sickly sounding pause,
Methought I heard some old man of the earth
Bewailing earthly loves'
(I, 438ff).

There is no scope here for outlining or speculating upon the reasons for the changes, but it is clear that we have two versions of the Fall which, if they contain the same themes and many of the same lines, are of radically different implication and mood. *The Fall of Hyperion* is no longer the story of a Fall in a larger context of perfectibility, although that context, to be represented by Apollo, was never actually realised in verse, but the lament for the fallen and the apparent recognition that Apollo can never be defined. In the first version Apollo could not be realised for reasons which we may speculate upon endlessly, reasons artistic and personal to Keats's life at this juncture; in the second version the door was closed for his appearance from the very outset, since Keats (or a poet-figure related to Keats) himself appeared in the poem and it was he who was to have been Apollo.

We may conclude of the *Hyperions*, however, as we concluded of *Kubla Khan*, and as one could not conclude so readily before the appearance of Romantic theories and preoccupations, that the fragment may have its own paradoxical completeness. The fact that Apollo cannot be presented as a convincing mythological figure to continue either version is indicative of the fact that the symbol of Apollo is now outmoded, has been surpassed by his reality. In *The Fall of Hyperion* Keats has experienced and embodied in poetry his experience of 'the agony' the strife of human hearts', he is in no sense now a mere 'dreaming thing' and is capable of reconciling beauty, truth, and passion. Apollo, this reconciliation, is no longer to be dreamed of as a distant goal; his essence has come so to pervade the poetry that it follows of necessity that, when the mythic conception formally requires him to appear in full dress, there is nothing to be said, for he has already appeared in another more diffused form.

*   *   *

These seem to me among the more influential and significant of Romantic versions of the Fall.[20] Their direction is away from the biblical towards a more generalised view of the myth. The analysis of a critical action with an important but debatable voluntary element gives way to a lyrical impression of contrast between the fallen and the unfallen. Perhaps the inability to write convincing drama is parallel to this abandonment of the clash of free will and necessity. The Fall myth veers towards being used as an interpretation of the peculiar state of the artist (representative in various ways and degrees of man in general) with his heightened sense of the disparity between what he sees and what he feels he more ideally ought to be able to see. Clearly the list of works which might be considered as versions of this more generalised theme is virtually endless, but I think we may see here a further development of the tendency to personalise the biblical myth, to see in it a recurrent situation as it affects the artist or man as seen by the artist.

And these versions involve the reader in a new way, for, as Shelley defines it, poetry now 'administers to the effect by acting upon the cause'; if we are sensitive, if we can take part in the existence of the sparrow, if we can leave ourselves, we have and can develop imagination, for 'the great secret of morals is love, or a going out of our nature, and an identification of ourselves with the beautiful which exists in thought, action, or person not our own.' The going out of ourselves seems to involve the artist's entering into himself to produce that with which we are to identify, the shaped product of his deepest experience, for which he makes a special claim and in the forming of which he may cut himself off or feel cut off from those for whom at least in part he writes. The entering into the work is something different from what is involved in the reading of the Old English poem or of Spenser; it is nearer what is involved in accepting a doctrine, virtually an act of belief. Literature is intensified, but narrowed. It *is*, but we have to plan our defences carefully if we dare to say it may *mean*.

6. Lord of the Flies

'Civilisation has forgotten that there is a difference between a puzzle and a mystery'
—William Golding

In his later works Golding's main characters have been artists of a sort, creating their imagined worlds in tension with the world around them, sometimes broken in an attempt to relate the two, and yet finding the effort ultimately worthwhile. Why do they find it worthwhile? What is revealed of their nature and of all human nature in the process? What reality is it which they face in disaster? These are questions to which in the apparent view of Golding there can only be answers of a limited sort.

The sort of answer we may expect to find takes us for the moment away from the Fall, and back to the nature of myth itself. For, whether he is concerned with the Fall, with Prometheus, with Neanderthal Man, or with Balder and Loki, there seems to run through Golding's novels a peculiarly modern myth which we have seen germinating in Romantic versions. I use the word 'myth' now in a loose popular sense, suggesting a recurrent pattern of thought and conclusion which acts as a continuing premise. I mean here a myth of the rejection of reductive patterns, for reasons enshrined in T. S. Eliot's *East Coker*—the search for the nature of being by concretely realised situations, the evolving towards a point where there can be no conclusions, where any conceptual conclusion appears inadequate and imposed, where all must be manifested and 'realised'.[1] It would be tedious to comment on the many ways in which this myth typifies our time and our sense of an existentialist vitality and integrity, however precarious, the rejection of classified experience in favour of the spontaneous, the cumulative and painful processes of experience, which we must all go through in order to achieve that insight which allows us to reject them or to understand them. In the spectacle of a man, particularly delineated and in a fully dramatic setting, facing not a crisis of events but the self which a crisis of events forces him to face, we are to understand that we learn something peculiar, which cannot be stated in conceptual terms, about our predicament, a predicament still viewed as the median state, but where hell is the unrelieved and incommunicable self, and heaven a state of peace arising from the indefinably right attitude to reality.

The greatness of a literary work on this view depends partly on the fullness of the realisation of the character or characters as they interact with the outside world, and partly on the fullness and conviction or plausibility with which are presented the systems and patterns which finally will be seen, with something of a shock, to be inadequate and distorting. They will be balanced at a tension, one against the other, very often, in a comprehensive and insoluble enigma; commitment is one-sided 'preaching'. None of these patterns is 'the answer', and their corporate embodiment is its own and only definition, which may be 'significant' indeed but cannot be in any way prescriptive, for that would be for the 'moral' to 'obtrude too openly'. There is a curious and painful conflict here; as the artist falls back on the relative certainty of the subjective, of personal experience embodied, so the requirement is for objectivity and the banishment of the self from his work and interpretation.

There may be profound implication in the emergence of this notion or at least in its critical recognition. For reduction, pattern, generalisation and conclusion, if necessarily partial and inaccurate, are difficult, dangerous, yet necessary to sane social existence, and the prevalence of this myth may point to a hollowness and falsity in society itself, and a deep gulf between the individual, as we would ideally see him, and society itself. The main direction of our literature and our criticism seems often to be away from these social functions to the private revelation, the exclusive preserve of individuals. So far as criticism goes, there is something disarming in the repeated fear—for all its analytical pages—of being mistaken for a substitute for the unique 'creative' work it not only cannot, by its own logic, replace, but whose existence it dare not presume to define, on whose territory it may have tiptoed, but on whose 'real' nature it cannot do more than shed a little finally irrelevant light. We murder to dissect; but we do so, and then point with wonder to the mysterious inviolate essence outside whose door we may with luck by dissection hope to arrive. But that is always a little further on. 'Quick, said the bird, find them/Round the corner'. We may even go in. But we cannot go in together; we can do no more than hope that others have been into the same place, although their perceptions must differ because we are individuals.

I am far from feeling that this belief is unsound or fallacious, or that it can be avoided. I feel only that it is of no demonstrable truth, as liable to pass away as the leaves on the tree. I feel also that its wholesale propagation can lead to a sense of futility in the critical proceeding related to a lack of value-consciousness outside. The beliefs of the author may be nothing to do with us, may not be identifiable with beliefs expressed, if any indirectly are expressed, in his poem or his novel, but they are nonetheless forms of beliefs, and our own beliefs and those of others are of great importance. It is very sane to allow life and art to be confused a little. Moreover, the consideration of literature as an isolated autotelic phenomenon is itself an expression of belief, even religious belief, or disbelief. Pater observed that poetry 'aspires towards the condition of music', not that it is music.[2] It is a mixed art, and it cannot cut itself off from inartistic activities, or be allowed in any stereotyped way to point beyond them. That is its strength as well as its weakness.

We are in our reading liable to be governed by this myth, and Golding's work pays a good deal of tribute to it. But is *Lord of the Flies* one of those inclusive works in which a situation is wholly dramatised, which cannot be 'reduced' to patterns and themes (or 'propositions' as Golding says in one of his several discussions of the question, in *The Brass Butterfly*)? Not, I think, entirely. And this is one of the main problems in assessing it or even reading it. For its deficiencies on the contingent, realistic, level, which are fairly plain in some aspects of style, dialogue, and contrivance, are just what cause us to consider it alongside a myth in the fuller sense of a situation enshrining beliefs held to be of a certain validity. The pattern is a reduction of the complex uncertainties of the work, of course, but it has at once entered into the work and remained intractable. It will always appear a pattern and the situation will appear a situation. At the present time the result strikes us as a qualified success, makes us uneasy; and yet, without the sense of the pattern, this would be but a slight and rather unrealistic skit on juvenile mannerisms in an improbable setting.

Pincher Martin is a specific individual, and this is essential for us to interest ourselves in him and for us to understand how his mind can build up a mini-Creation around and within itself. It is a legend that at the moment of drowning, the events of one's life flash before one's mental eyes; but I do not suppose for one moment that many of us imagine that we shall make such a review as Pincher makes. Inasmuch as he is specified and uncommonly articulate, to that extent his situation veers away from the typical situation of the drowned man surveying his life, the soul in a purgatory of its own making, a delayed self-realisation to give sense to a life which is over. The schoolboys on the island are also individuals, and their world recognisably that of a twentieth-century private-schoolboy. That is essential to our realising the realities of which mythic patterns are made, but it is not essential to the pattern. There is something more typical and less specific in Prometheus or even in the Adams and Eves we have seen, who are by no means devoid of individuality and social context than in Jocelyn of *The Spire*. There is not a direct clash with the established myth. But the specific is held in some sort of relationship, at times it may seem an awkward one, with the outline of mythic thought to which the author, in his themes, is partly committed. We cannot say that the pattern came first and he dressed it up. Neither can we say that the situation came first and appeared to evince a pattern. What we can say is that the two are not entirely one.

*   *   *

The parallel or contrast with *The Coral Island* of R. M. Ballantyne, though much discussed, seems to me of limited interest, though it may direct us. Ballantyne's book deals with boys establishing a minimal society (just about) and 'making a go' of an apparently hopeless predicament. They succeed in this both because the author has decided that it is in the nature of man—and particularly of late Victorian Englishman—to succeed in such things, and because the predicament is in fact very much less hopeless than it at first appears to be—the island is far more of a paradise and the egos of the boys are largely sunshine. The book belongs more with *Robinson Crusoe* and similar visions. It implies a view of human nature and that optimistic view is certainly part of its myth, with which Golding takes issue. But the origins of sin and evil, though sin and evil plainly confront the boys and will be overcome maybe by the missionary society, are not part of that myth. By contrast, they are the subject of *Lord of the Flies*, which has its paradise less glossy than the one in *Coral Island*, and substitutes a partly subjective or relativistic viewpoint whereby the paradise is created by the eye of the beholder—and the eyes of these beholders are less jovial than those of Ballantyne's Ralph. Whatever it set out to do, *Lord of the Flies* can hardly impugn the limited myth of *Coral Island*, which is one of the eternal childlike dreams, and, more importantly, the realisation, the style, the reality of the dialogue, and the author's voice are not vital to the success of Ballantyne's book. It purports only in a very tangential way to deal with reality. It is in no sense an analysis of reality although in a limited sense it may be a prescriptive criticism of reality as the author sees it.

Just because *Lord of the Flies* penetrates this dream which cannot be destroyed, aspects of style are more important to the later work. If the one substitutes a dream for reality, the other seems to make some claim to substitute reality for the dream. But, because it also appeals to the myth of Original Sin, and the vexed question of Original Guilt, so they relate the book to the lasting and mythic rather than to the temporal and contingent. Style, therefore, in *Lord of the Flies* works in two contrasted directions. This is not, despite its criticism of the dream, a fully realistic account of schoolboys reacting to a situation—the sketchiness of the perimeter and precipitating circumstances confirm that it is not so. On the contrary, the question is of credibility rather than of realism, and this is a far more difficult and subjective matter on which to comment.

The crucial issue is our being led in the course of the book to take on a view of human nature, with whatever qualifications, with which, being predisposed to think in terms of the *Coral Island* paradise and pastoral idylls generally, we do not start out. Since the book starts in a chummy manner which establishes the false dream, we wish to discover by the end just how this change has been arranged; our attention is forced to the art because we sense that we have been manipulated. In the same way we wish to find out precisely when, to our initial astonishment, Pincher Martin died, or with Sammy Mountjoy of *Free Fall* to isolate the occasion when freedom was lost. What we want to discover, having rejected the beast and all external objects to blame, is precisely when the evils in the hearts of the schoolboys were first manifested. And it has been designed that this is the one thing we cannot do. If no such moment can be found—and none can—we are thrown on to a different level, the style ensures, on to an absent God, or at least on to a mystery which research into parents' psychologies will only turn into an infinite series. With the semi-realism of the schoolboy capers, then, there goes a style to suggest a religious dimension by which man is both more essentially evil than the average reader readily admits (though 'Belsen and Hiroshima have gone some way towards teaching us humility')[3] and is less responsible for his actions and their outcome.

If this is a theme, the book is as much about the necessity for an original Fall as it is about the reenactment of a Fall which it purports to be. It is certainly close to the Romantic indefinable catastrophe to which we are repeatedly subject, but it is close also to the 'threshold' state of the minds of Eve and the Red Cross Knight in their warning dreams; it concerns the passage of evil through the mind before and after confirmation by acts of will, and so governing behaviour that the precise moment when an act of will occurs is ever obscure. The aggressiveness of schoolboy games and wordplay changes by imperceptible and apparently inevitable stages to the real thing. You cannot pinpoint the moment when the frontier is crossed, if indeed there is a frontier.[4] Who is to say how much of human will lies in the sportive actions of Ralph as he 'returned as a fighter-plane, with wings swept back, and machine-gunned Piggy'? (p. 11) When we give up the 'puzzle' we find it a 'mystery', and there is presumed a value in fully knowing mystery.

*　*　*

Golding's novels seem to aim towards realisation, a self-realisation in one or more principal characters, and a realisation slightly later in the reader, which may or may not precisely accord with that in the characters. To this end, his art is an art of revelation, a technique of concealment which at times looks awkwardly like the machinations of a pot-boiler's plot. We see it in the case of Pincher Martin's death, the delay of the final school scenes in *Free Fall*, the finally revealed death of Pangall in *The Spire*, the fate of Liku in *The Inheritors*. It is a tactical and technical device. They are books carefully planned, if much revised, so that for much of them the author knows more than his reader. In *Lord of the Flies* this device is widespread but not obtrusive, except perhaps in the case of the parachutist, and in this first novel it is more in the characterisation than in the plot as such. Frequently, and particularly of course in the Assemblies, we seem invited to choose between the views of the main characters, invited to make an alliance with one or other of them, which later events will not permit us to do. It is central to the conception that the characters do not change so much as reveal themselves, their true natures. We peel off, in Eliot's phrase, the layers of the onion. And if, for the most part, we do not in ordinary life display these true natures—that is another matter, granted that, nonetheless, the world at large is engaged in atomic warfare and is not regarded as very admirable.

Take the case of Ralph, who from the first is slightly aloof as a character, and with whom the book both begins and ends.

> 'Jack started to protest but the clamour changed from the general wish for a chief to an election by acclaim of Ralph himself. None of the boys could have found good reason for this; what intelligence had been shown was traceable to Piggy while the obvious leader was Jack. But there was a stillness about Ralph as he sat that marked him out: there was his size, and attractive appearance; and most obscurely, yet most powerfully, there was the conch. The being that had blown that, had sat waiting for them on the platform with the delicate thing balanced on his knees, was set apart' (p. 22).[5]

The 'apartness' of Ralph, different from the apartness of Piggy, makes him the choice as leader. He had indeed blown the conch, but it was not so much his idea as Piggy's:

> '"We can use this to call the others. Have a meeting. They'll come when they hear us . . ."
> He beamed at Ralph.
> "That was what you meant, didn't you? That's why you got the conch out of the water?"'

It wasn't what Ralph meant in fact—he thought of it more as an 'interesting and worthy plaything'. Events reveal that Ralph the opportunist is ideally a better democratic leader than Jack, but he lacks the essential decisiveness and personal power. He decides that shelters are needed not only from the rain which may return, but because the littluns are frightened, a fact which Jack has dimly noticed but which he comments upon with a contemptuous 'They're batty' (p. 50). Again,

> '"Only Ralph says you scream in the night. What does that mean but nightmares? Anyway, you don't build or help or hunt—you're a lot of cry-babies and sissies, that's what. And as for fear—you'll have to put up with that like the rest of us."
> Ralph looked at Jack open-mouthed, but Jack took no notice. "The thing is—fear can't hurt you any more than a dream. There aren't any beasts to be afraid of in this island"' (p. 79).[6]

Already there are the differences which will emerge in Jack's reign of terror and Ralph's impotence as leader. And already, after the quarrels of the assemblies and the smashing of Piggy's glasses, Ralph is aware within himself of some disaster working itself out and destroying his orderly paradise, 'the imagined but never fully realised place leaping into real life' (p. 15). The littluns' fear of the 'beastie or snake-thing' is not only greeted with some understanding by him but tends towards the confirming of this inner fear—'As if this wasn't a good island. Yes, that's right.' Pondering on 'the imagined but never fully realised place' of his first expedition into the interior, Ralph

> 'found himself understanding the wearisomeness of this life, where every path was an improvisation and a considerable part of one's waking life was spent watching one's feet. He stopped, facing the strip; and remembering that first enthusiastic exploration as though it were part of a brighter childhood, he smiled jeeringly'
>
> (p. 72).

This solitary reflection precedes, is even the cause of, the break-up of the critical assembly meeting which follows, in which he is unable to maintain his leadership and cannot muster confidence in his own qualities:

> '"If I blow the conch and they don't come back; then we've had it. We shan't keep the fire going. We'll be like animals. We'll never be rescued."
> "If you don't blow, we'll soon be animals anyway"'
>
> (p. 88).

He cannot make up his mind between possible courses of action—

> 'Was it better to fetch Piggy's glasses, or would the ship have gone? Or if they climbed on, supposing the fire was right out, and they had to watch Piggy crawling nearer and the ship sinking under the horizon? Balanced on a high peak of need, agonised by indecision, Ralph cried out "Oh God, Oh God!"'
>
> (p. 64).

There are so many factors to consider and he has no scale by which to assess them. Increasingly he is numbed by the sense that 'Things are breaking up. I don't understand why. We began well; we were happy. And then people started getting frightened. But that's littluns' talk'. In the disintegrating society where every possibility is of equal importance he is a good thinker but no decider:

> 'By now Ralph had no self-consciousness in public thinking, but would treat the day's decisions as though he were playing chess. The only trouble was that he would never be a very good chess player. He thought of the littluns and Piggy. Vividly he imagined Piggy by himself, huddled in a shelter that was silent except for the sounds of nightmare'
>
> (p. 112).

It is repeatedly Ralph, supported by his finally lamented friend Piggy, who keeps the ideas of smoke and fire before the group's minds as needed to secure rescue. But in this sense they are straws to clutch at—he does not let them change in his mind as the situation changes, whereas Jack, after letting the main fire out, needs to light a small one for his own hunters expressly to cook by. Ralph retains a conscience—he, like Piggy, finds excuses for their participation in the dance in which Simon was killed. He sticks by 'law and rescue' rather than 'hunting and breaking things up', yet he gradually approaches the savagery of Jack and his tribe, Then he cannot understand why, as he plays almost a double part, they cannot accept him as harmless. In the battle with Jack's second raiding party

> 'Ralph twisted sideways on top of the writhing body and felt hot breath on his cheek. He began to pound the mouth below him, using his clenched fist as a hammer; he hit with more and more passionate hysteria as the face became slippery'
>
> (p. 159).

He remarks with satisfaction of that moment, 'I gave one of 'em what for. I smashed him up alright . . .' Later he descends fully to the level of the savages, but as the victim, the man on the wrong side of the fence, broken down from his true stature by necessity:

> 'He squatted back on his heels and showed his teeth at the wall of branches. He raised his spear, snarled a little, and waited . . . Ralph launched himself like a cat; stabbed snarling with the spear, and the savage doubled up'.
>
> (p. 185).

Ralph has, almost from the first, a vague sense of something wrong, and it is something which he cannot get outside, something of which he is part. He cannot entirely resign his belief, supported by Piggy, that 'decent' behaviour will right it or set limits on it. He accompanies Piggy in the climactic embassy to Jack's men, the fatal final testing of the conch and the quest for Piggy's glasses to be given back 'because what's right's right'. He is broken down and hunted, but he achieves even then no self-realisation until the end of the book when the tones of the officer show to both us and him that the decent civilisation which he has valued may be of limited value and limited genuineness. Then it is a realisation which (if possessed from the start) could not have helped him in his hunted predicament.

> 'The tears began to flow and sobs shook him. He gave him-
> self up to them now for the first time on the island; great,
> shuddering spasms of grief seemed to wrench his whole
> body. His voice rose under the black smoke before the
> burning wreckage of the island; and infected by that
> emotion, the other little boys began to shake and sob too.
> And in the middle of them, with filthy body, matted hair,
> and unwiped nose, Ralph wept for the end of innocence,
> the darkness of man's heart, and the fall through the air of
> the true wise friend called Piggy'
>
> (p. 192).

We are not in a position to question Ralph's values in realistic terms. We can see only that they do not help the extreme situation in which he finds himself. It is an open, if important, problem, as to whether they fit any other situation. For what Ralph comes to realise is something unpalatable—whether or not the 'darkness of man's heart' materially affects the normal business of life. Whether Ralph benefits by it one can hardly say, but I take it that the main 'proposition' of the novel, insofar as there is one, is that the recognition and the process of recognising are valuable experiences, more valuable than the precisely definable nature of what is recognised, and this seems to me the personal myth having a distinct bearing on the form and nature of the book over and above the analysis of evil and sin.

*   *   *

With the civilised and handsome Ralph is contrasted from the first the ordinary but compelling personality of Jack Merridrew, and again it is a case of gradual revelation, followed by a fairly sudden plunge into the depths of character, rather than of actively changing character. Jack, a 'tall, thin, bony' boy, his face 'crumpled, freckled, and ugly without silliness', is possessed of a conscience together with the strong aggressive drive by which we perhaps tend to remember him most clearly. He is second to none in the 'shame' and excuses which he feels and offers for stabbing or not stabbing the first pig which is encountered, and, indeed, often throughout the book we are made aware that the sense of guilt and the impulse to sin go together, as do the necessary domination of self-preservation and leadership and the destructive urge of sadism.

'He raised his arm in the air. There came a pause, a hiatus, the pig continued to scream and the creepers to jerk, and the blade continued to flash at the end of a bony arm. The pause was only long enough for them to understand what an enormity the downward stroke would be. The piglet tore loose from the creepers and scurried into the undergrowth. They were left looking at each other and the place of terror. Jack's face was white under the freckles. He noticed that he still held the knife aloft and brought his arm down replacing the blade in the sheath. Then they all three laughed ashamedly and began to climb back to the track. "I was choosing a place", said Jack. "I was waiting for a moment to decide where to stab him . . ."

They knew very well why he hadn't; because of the enormity of the knife descending and cutting into living flesh; because of the unbearable blood.

"I was going to", said Jack. He was ahead of them and they could not see his face. "I was choosing a place. Next time . . .!"'

(p. 30).

Jack is of the type who cannot distinguish shame and cowardice. Their knowledge of his 'weakness' is for him a 'dare' to steel himself.

He wants rules to satisfy his need for assertion and to give him the vicarious pleasure of pain if they are broken ('We'll have rules. Lots of rules! Then when anyone breaks them . . .'). He adheres to the procedure with the conch so long as it suits him, but abandons the arbitrary organisation when it works against his own interest in being on top, which will not be flouted. Whilst he observes the decorum, he speaks in a way remarkably similar to that of the officer at the end of the book, displaying the kinship of this child society with the adult one of greed and atom bombs;

> 'Jack held out his hands for the conch and stood up, holding the delicate thing carefully in his sooty hands. "I agree with Ralph. We've got to have rules and obey them. After all, we're not savages. We're English; and the English are best at everything. So we've got to do the right things"'
>
> (p. 41).

In the case of Jack it is plain that civilised behaviour, itself a limited virtue, is a conditioned layer, which he is capable of exploiting for his own ends, over the deeper and more primitive self. Next it will be 'Bollocks to the rules! We're strong. We hunt! If there's a beast we'll hunt it down! We'll close in and beat and beat and beat.' At the idea of hunting there comes into his eyes a 'mad opaque look' (of which we hear a good deal more) by which Ralph, so different, is bewildered. It was a 'compulsion to track down and kill that was swallowing him up', a compulsion he can neither explain nor control. His likeness to a predatory animal is very early stressed, whereas it is not until near the end that Ralph becomes the hunted;

> 'He lowered his chin and stared at the traces as though he would force them to speak to him. Then doglike, uncom-

fortably on all fours, he stole forward five yards and
stopped . . . Jack crouched with his face a few inches
away from this clue, then stared forward into the semi-
darkness of the undergrowth. A sharpened stick about five
feet long trailed from his right hand; and except for a pair
of tattered shorts held up by his knife-belt he was naked.
He closed his eyes, raised his head and breathed in gently
with flared nostrils, assessing the current of warm air for
information'

(p. 46).

At first he indeed assents to the idea of the fire as a rescue-
signal, and it is he, the man of action, whom, 'the conch forgotten', the boys follow to put this plan into effect. But within
twenty pages the plan also is forgotten:

'Jack had to think a moment before he could remember
what rescue was. "Rescue? Yes, of course! All the same,
I'd like to catch a pig first—." He snatched up his spear
and dashed it into the ground. The opaque, mad look came
into his eyes again . . .'

(p. 51).

And he forgets about the rescue and the possible ship, crying
out 'Got it!' at cross-purposes with Ralph as Ralph says in
anger, 'All you can talk about is pig, pig, pig!' So he lets the
fire go out at the crucial moment when a ship has been sighted
because he has hunted a pig. The desire to kill becomes a
primitive lust, not without sexual associations,[7] and, it seems
suggested, perhaps some primordial drive from his ancestors—

'His mind was crowded with memories; memories of the
knowledge which had come to them when they had closed
in on the struggling pig, knowledge that they had outwitted
a living thing, imposed their will upon it, taken its life like
a long satisfying drink'

(p. 67).

Jack's plunge into savagery occurs when he paints himself and dances, snarling as Ralph finally snarls. It is a means of camouflage from the hunted pigs primarily. But it has other associations. 'Like in the war. You know—dazzle—paint. Like things trying to look like something else . . .' Soldiers are he-men. The paint releases him from the irksome feelings of conscience, responsibility and order, which have hitherto complicated his will to dominate. 'The mask was a thing on its own, behind which Jack hid, liberated from shame and self-consciousness.' For he and Ralph both fight a battle with 'self-consciousness'; and it is perhaps to be expected that, artistically, a type struggling for individuality should have to fight such a battle.

But, long before this step has been taken, he and Ralph have proved incompatible, disputing leadership on every occasion. The book presents a series of encounters between them of gradually mounting intensity, until Jack's lot break away, Jack becomes an 'idol' on a log, and finally, though Ralph cannot comprehend their hostility still ('What have I done? I liked him . . .'), the enmity becomes a life-and-death battle between them. There is no meaningful communication. Their appeals to each other, even their short-lived agreements, are a sort of truce, always motivated, Ralph's by what he, the chess-player, conceives to be for the good of the whole, Jack's by what he considers to be in the interests of himself as potential leader.

Ralph's sights are on rescue and return to society. They are futuristic, even long-term to a fault. The most the boys can do, in his estimation, is to palliate the present predicament with shelters and a fire (which is to give security to the littluns at night as well as to be a rescue-signal). This is the conclusion of his long reflection before the third assembly. He is a thinker who will not resign thought and yet sees that it is not enough—even though for him this is a 'strange mood of speculation':

'Again he lost himself in deep waters . . . The trouble was, if you were a chief you had to think, you had to be wise. And then the occasion slipped by so that you had to grab at a decision. This made you think; because thought was a valuable thing, that got results . . .'

(p. 74).

Jack is not a thinker at all in this sense. The 'interim, the hideous dream' is no trouble to him. He forms an idea and then immediately sets about enforcing it. He has no long-term plan save an instinctive consistency. He will make the best of a bad job, even make it a good job in his own way, and 'have fun' such as circumstances permit, a hedonism which holds no interest for Ralph. His own nature has convinced him that hunting and feeding, with the pleasure of getting his way, are going to be a sufficient satisfaction for his time on the island.

Jack and Ralph are two types, even two philosophies, and they are not depicted as reconcilable; even with the eventual knowledge of the 'end of innocence, the darkness of man's heart', Ralph's maturity will bring him no nearer to the older Jack.

'They walked along, two continents of experience and feeling, unable to communicate. 'If only I could get a pig.' 'I'll come back and go on with the shelter!' They looked at each other, baffled, in love and hate'

(p. 53).

There is perhaps more of the hate than the love depicted in the novel. They are astonished 'at the rub of feeling' as they fall out with each other; but we are not, though we can understand the company's fascination in the development and eventual bursting of the subterranean antagonism—'the other boys forgot their urge to be gone and turned back to sample of the fresh rub of two spirits in the dark' (p. 114). The balance of sympathy is certainly against Jack, but on the whole the book does maintain some sort of balance whereby we see the two as in a measure both complementary and incompatible, the thinker deprived of action, the man of action deprived of thought and knowledge.

*   *   *

Ralph, if he is viewed more favourably than Jack, is in no sense an ideal. He has within him, as we see in his gradual falling into savagery, or his misjudged eagerness to hit the boar in Chapter 7, the same hunting drives as Jack, though in a lesser degree. It was he who 'shrieked with laughter' at the revelation of Piggy's burdensome nickname, and he who 'returned as a fighter-plane, with wings swept back, and machine-gunned Piggy', just as it was he who, within a few pages, so underestimated Piggy's embarrassment at his name that he revealed the name to Jack.

Piggy himself would be incapable of such infidelity. He is a precocious, awkward boy, full of contradictions, totally without tact, over-adult for his age in a superficial sense, childish in his resentments and trusts. Yet he is shown above all as a faithful friend, thereby representing something so rare on the island that it is incorporated in the conclusion—'the fall through the air of the true wise friend called Piggy', though perhaps not without some irony at the name and the wisdom. Piggy desires as well as gives friendship; in fact, he has a desperate need for it—

'Piggy rubbed his glasses slowly and thought. When he understood how far Ralph had gone towards accepting him he flushed pinkly with pride'

(p. 133).

The loss of Piggy, even before the end, is part of Ralph's deepening vision of gloom.

'Piggy was everywhere, was on this neck, was become terrible in darkness and death. If Piggy were to come back now out of the water, with his empty head—Ralph whimpered and yawned like a littlun . . .'

(p. 181).

Piggy's death shatters all remaining faith in the conch as talisman, and, characteristically naive as is his appeal to Jack to return his glasses, and his faith in the conch until it is broken, we are made to feel that something of great value is destroyed both in the conch and in Piggy. The conch is indeed but an emblem; Jack truly observes that it has no power at his end of the island; and neither Ralph nor Piggy realises to what an extent its power is purely relative to the power of those who use it. But Piggy's views, for all their oversimplification, have some unshakable merit. 'We know what goes on and if there's something wrong, there's someone to put it right.' He decides that there is not a beast—'not with claws and all that, I mean.' The fear of the beast can be ignored, but with the important qualification that that is only 'unless we get frightened of people'. The fear of people and the domination of people go hand in hand, and they are an integral part of the evil on the island.

Piggy, so peculiarly adult for his age, has before him always adults as an ideal, and in them he places a very unadult reliance. As he is repeatedly shouted down in the assemblies his voice 'lifted in a whine of virtuous recrimination'. For Piggy is more annoyed than frightened that the real world around him does not correspond with his expectations, is not what the world on his calculations should be. The power-world is totally beyond his comprehension. His view of adults is that they are divorced from children, have no childlike elements in them. They are all but the scientific machines which he also worships—'if there's something wrong, there must be someone to put it right'; what goes up must come down. 'Grown-ups know things. They ain't afraid of the dark. They'd meet and have tea and discuss. Then things'd be alright.' Twice he compares the whole company with the adult world which he imagines so different. He even includes Ralph in his disgust as they busy themselves seeking firewood 'like a crowd of kids', 'like a pack of kids'. But his thick glasses, and the breaking of them, represent plainly enough, perhaps too plainly, the 'myopia' of his insight into the actual situation before him.

In practical matters Piggy is useless. He is 'indignant', 'whining', when accused of neglecting his special charge of counting the children, though he repeatedly accuses the others of carelessness over the disappearance of the boy with the birthmark. Then there is his asthma, of which the reader wearies as much as do the rest of the boys by the end of the book. For Piggy is loaded with every possible defect to compensate for his bookish wisdom and illusory adulthood. His claim that Simon 'was batty. He asked for it' to come crouching into the ring of frightened hunters after dark may have some justice (indeed, it does, for Simon's vision is also limited), but it is Piggy who wheedles out of responsibility for murdering Simon and tries to convince Ralph and Sam of their substantial innocence of the crime. We recognise here the 'whining' (the repeated word for Piggy) sneak:

> '"And look, Ralph". Piggy glanced round quickly, then leaned close—"don't let on we was in that dance. Not to Samneric."
> "But we were! All of us!"
> Piggy shook his head.
> "Not us till last. They never noticed in the dark. Anyway you said I was only on the outside—"
> "So was I," muttered Ralph, "I was on the outside too."
> Piggy nodded eagerly.
> "That's right. We was on the outside. We never done nothing, we never seen nothing"'
>
> (p. 149).

But, when all the qualifications and objections have been raised (and they are many), the fact remains that Piggy possesses an intelligence, sometimes a sense of what is feasible, and a faith in the powers of mind—not to mention a distinctive Cockney dialect—that no other boy possesses. He has, moreover three further positive qualities—the martyr's ambiguous faith in what he dies for (the conch, his glasses, a code of decent behaviour), the partial accuracy of his conclusion on the nature of the beast, and his friendship with Ralph. These are weighty things to mitigate irritating defects.

∗   ∗   ∗

Finally among the 'biguns' who appear to hold an answer to the situation is Simon, Simon who by age is a 'middlun' and whom we only see at length twice. Simon is, as we have seen, in Piggy's view 'batty', and by the others he is variously termed 'queer', 'funny' and 'cracked'. He is an outsider, and for him Golding reserves a special kind of prose which associates him with the vision of a cosmic order outside and over both the chaotic worlds of the island and the war-torn earth at large.

The littluns viewed with contempt as a nuisance by Jack and rather as a necessary evil, but with some compassion, by Ralph, are to Simon as the needy poor.

> 'Then, amid the roar of bees in the afternoon sunlight, Simon found for them the fruit they could not reach, pulled off the choicest from up in the foliage, passed them back down to the endless, outstretched hands. When he had satisfied them he paused and looked round. The littluns watched him inscrutably over double handfuls of ripe fruit'
>
> (p. 54).

Parts of the island are for him a paradise where 'flower and fruit grew together on the same tree and everywhere was the scent of ripeness.' He finds a little bower among the creepers where he disappears to look at the sights and listen to the sounds of the island. There is room for the mystery of gradual processes in Simon's vision, which distinguishes itself sharply from the increasing bustle of the rest:

> 'Evening was advancing towards the island; the sounds of the bright fantastic birds, the bee-sounds, even the crying

of the gulls that were returning to their roosts among the square rocks, were fainter. The deep sea breaking miles away on the reef made an undertone less perceptible than the susurration of the blood . . . With the fading of the light the riotous colours died and the heat and urgency cooled away. The candle-buds stirred. Their green carpels drew back a little and the white tips of the flowers rose delicately to meet the open air.

Now the sunlight had lifted clear of the open space and withdrawn from the sky. Darkness poured out, submerging the ways between the trees till they were dim and strange as the bottom of the sea. The candle-buds opened their wide white flowers glimmering under the light that pricked down from the stars. Their scent spilled out into the air and took possession of the island'

(p. 55).

The candle-buds, from *Coral Island*, hold no interest for anyone but Simon, who identifies them. No one else sees them open. They have the worst defect of the beautiful on the island—they are useless; '"You couldn't light them", said Ralph, "They just look like candles." "Green candles", said Jack contemptuously, "We can't eat them. Come on"' (p. 30).

Simon's insight, whatever its value or its truth, is of no practical nature. Moreover, he has his shortcomings as does Piggy; he is nervous, diffident, subject to fits. His climactic vision of the Lord of the Flies itself takes place during one of these 'times'. Yet his vision is more endorsed by the novelist's writing than is any other.

As Ralph surveys the ocean, the 'ceaseless, bulging passage of the deep sea waves', with breakers 'less a progress than a momentous rise and fall of the whole ocean', 'something of the remoteness of the sea numbed his brain', and he is overcome by the feeling that 'this was the divider, the barrier', too wide to be crossed, destroying all his hopes of rescue. Simon, unlike Ralph, is equal to this vision, and he defies him (and the reader at this

moment) with the notion that all shall be well; 'You'll get back
to where you came from . . . You'll get back alright. I think
so, anyway . . .' It may be so; Simon's vision is the sole one
on the side of optimism in the book (if we discount, as we surely
must, the utopian words of Piggy). It answers no urgent
questions; yet it is distinctive and positive, and it is irreconcilable
with the indecisiveness of Ralph, the savagery of Jack, and the
curious second-hand wisdom of Piggy. It has but one drawback,
to be considered in a moment; its linguistic virtuosity is such that
we have a nasty feeling that in talking of the sea as 'the divider, the
barrier', in the conscious visionary rhapsody, Simon almost seems
to suggest that the sea is that which one must cross with Tenny-
son to see one's Pilot face to face. It is, in a word, overdone.

When the issue of the 'beastie' is dramatically revived by the
twins' having seen the parachutist floating down—the ironical
sign from the grown-up world for which Ralph had prayed—it is
Simon who insists that this must be investigated. Simon, who
has already become 'inarticulate in his effort to express mankind's essential illness',[8] had suggested that the beast is 'maybe
only us' and seen 'in his inward sight the picture of a human at
once heroic and sick'. The wish to investigate is quite consistent.
Simon had only glimpsed these interpretations and they were
not certainties to him. He is not going to the mountain to check
up on them or confirm them. He wishes merely to discover the
truth, and he knows that the truth and the beast are unaccountably related. The truth is not that the beast does not exist or can
be discounted, but that it is not outside the people but inside
them. Certainly it is not a pig's head stuck on a stick as a totem,
a propitiation for some other beast (the 'theological speculation'
comes to Jack that they should 'keep on the right side of him
anyhow'), nor is it a primitive devil or merely a primordial
drive. As Simon hears it, it is rather a sophisticated voice, something very like the voice of the naval officer at the end, or of his
schoolmaster:

'"You knew, didn't you? I'm part of you? Close, close,

close. I'm the reason why it's no go? Why things are what
they are? I'm warning you. I'm going to get waxy . . .
We are going to have fun on this island. So don't try it on,
my poor misguided boy, or else . . ."'

(p. 137).

The beast—at least as Simon hears it when 'one of his times was
coming on'—is at once the aggressive unconditioned drives
within each of the boys, and also the civilised, conditioning
force itself with which they are at war.

Simon, after inspecting the parachutist which 'breathed
foully at him', having experienced this complex evil, 'was sick
till his stomach was empty', as Neanderthal Man, in *The
Inheritors*, is sick after partaking of the beverages of Homo
Sapiens. Finally he crawls back to the tribe and is brutally
murdered in the ritual dance. This, we are perhaps to suppose,
is a price the visionary pays for his unwelcome insight. Simon is
a conscience which must be destroyed. It is also a demonstration
that 'I'm part of you', that 'the beast is maybe only us'. It is the
half-predictable fate of one who was an outsider, who crawled
back, as Ralph will crawl back, to the tribe. 'He was batty. He
asked for it.'

*   *   *

Simon is unique in the book. There are no clear parallels or
contrasts with him, as Jack and Ralph are paralleled and
contrasted. But his death of course contrasts very markedly with
that of Piggy and each receives a style appropriate to his ideals.
The Piggy who 'discounted learnedly as a "mirage"' the glittering
sea, the land rising and falling, the palms quivering and running
'like raindrops on a wire', dies in a very stark and factual
manner:

'The rock bounded twice and was lost in the forest. Piggy
fell forty feet and landed on his back across that square

red rock in the sea. His head opened and stuff came out and turned red. Piggy's arms and legs twitched a bit, like a pig's after it has been killed. Then the sea breathed again in a long, slow sigh, the water boiled white and pink over the rock; and when it went, sucking back again, the body of Piggy was gone'

(p. 172).

Simon, the visionary for all his fits and inability to cope with society, is granted a transmutation in death, becoming one with the order beyond both microcosm and macrocosm which he and the author alone in the book can live with:

'The tide swelled in over the rain-pitted sand and smoothed everything with a layer of silver. Now it touched the first of the stains that seeped from the broken body and the creatures made a moving patch of light as they gathered at the edge. The water rose further and dressed Simon's coarse hair with brightness. The lines of his cheek silvered and the turn of his shoulder became sculptured marble. The strange attendant creatures, with their fiery eyes and trailing vapours busied themselves round his head . . . Somewhere over the darkened curve of the world the sun and moon were pulling; and the film of water on the earth planet was held, bulging slightly on one side while the solid core turned. The great tide moved further along the island and the water lifted. Softly, surrounded by a fringe of inquisitive bright creatures, itself a silver shape beneath the steadfast constellations, Simon's body moved out towards the open sea'

(p. 146).

'Bright', 'light', 'silver', 'fire'—these are the words reserved for Simon again and again. The other characters do not change, so much as reveal their natures stripped in special circumstances.

They are reduced. Simon, if his appearance alters at all, is not reduced but aggrandised, for all his ineffectiveness.

* * *

Corresponding to the gradual revelation of 'true' characters there is a continuous process of suggesting and then gradually bringing out the 'true' nature of situations and characters reflected in them. It is done largely by games and mimes which turn out later in the book to be re-enacted in reality. Obviously the case of Ralph's 'machine-gunning' Piggy is a case in point, indicating the annoyance everyone—including the reader—will feel with Piggy later on. A larger case is the rolling of rocks, evidently derived in part from the falling boulder in *Coral Island*.

In their first exploration of the island, when Ralph has 'expressed the intensity of his emotion by pretending to knock Simon down', the boys eventually succeed in loosening and rolling a vast rock down the hillside:

> 'The great rock loitered, poised on one toe, decided not to return, moved through the air, fell, struck, turned over, leapt droning through the air and smashed a deep hole in the canopy of the forest. Echoes and birds flew, white and pink dust floated, the forest further down shook as with the passage of an enraged monster; and then the island was still.
> "Wacco!"
> "Like a bomb!"
> "Whee-aa-oo!"
> Not for five minutes could they drag themselves away from this triumph'
>
> (p. 27).

The rock is personified, then it is compared to a monster, the crash is 'like a bomb', the noise 'Whee-aa-oo' is as the boys delightedly imagine the punishment which will follow the breaking of rules established in the first Assembly—'Whee-oh!' Then, as they set out for the mountain in search of the parachute beast, Ralph thinking all the time of the absence of the needed smoke-signal, they are diverted by the pleasure of rolling a large rock down into the sea, which Ralph cannot stop them doing. Finally, a great red rock is levered down on to Piggy and the conch, and further rocks are rolled down into the thicket to expose the hunted Ralph in his sanctuary before he, too, is about to be murdered.

In a small way the stone-throwing which started in pleasure at missing follows the same pattern. Roger casts stones at Henry but is prevented from aiming directly at him by 'the taboo of the old life', though that was 'conditioned by a civilisation that knew nothing of him and was in ruins'. Later, as Ralph and Piggy rely on the shell and try to recapture Piggy's spectacles from the tribe, 'Roger took up a small stone and flung it between the twins, aiming to miss. They started and Sam only just kept his footing. Some source of power began to pulse in Roger's body' (p. 167)—a source of power shortly to be fulfilled in the killing of Piggy by Roger with 'delirious abandonment.' Clearly there are suggested in these juvenile amusements the same transformation from person to monster which is undergone by that first rock, the same emotions, at the time harmless, as will issue in murders no less horrible for being committed in the heat of the blood and the rhythm of the dance rather than in cold calculation.

More lurid is the atmosphere surrounding the mock huntings.

'Then Maurice pretended to be the pig and ran squealing into the centre, and the hunters, circling still, pretended to beat him. As they danced they sang,
"Kill the pig. Cut her throat. Bash her in!"'

Ralph, contemplating calling an assembly, nevertheless watched this not only 'resentful' but also 'envious'. Presently, after the unsuccessful boar-hunt, Robert is the victim. Ralph is unable this time to resist and 'was fighting to get near, to get a handful of that brown, vulnerable flesh. The desire to squeeze and hurt was over-mastering . . . "Just a game", said Ralph uneasily.'

> '"You want a real pig", said Robert, still caressing his rump, "because you've got to kill him."
> "Use a littlun", said Jack, and everybody laughed.'
>
> (p. 110).

When the pig is killed, accompanied by sexual imagery,

> 'This time Robert and Maurice acted the two parts; and Maurice's acting of the pig's efforts to avoid the advancing spear was so funny that the boys cried with laughter'
>
> (p. 130).

Next time, though they devise excuses afterwards, 'Piggy and Ralph found themselves eager to take a place in this demented but partly secure society' of hunters. 'A thing was crawling out of the forest . . . It was crying out against the abominable noise something about a body on the hill', and Simon is the actual victim of the pig hunt, the beast who is exorcised. Climactically, if somewhat contrivedly, the winds blow and the rains fall and the parachute fills and moves away out to sea.

As the point about the characterisation—and it is very much a technique of characterisation—is that it is impossible to find any one characteristic which is responsible for 'the end of innocence', so the point about the games and mock hunts is that it is impossible to say at what point they become dangerous or excessive. They exhibit at the start, at their most trivial, the same urges as will eventually achieve realisation in killing, and those urges are common to all in the book except 'batty' Simon of whom we hardly see enough to judge. If these are children showing in a personal and small-scale manner what drives their adults to atomic warfare, the question arises as to when the destructive elements enter them. Are they in fact passed on by

that civilisation which is for many of them the standard of right-
ness, or are they inborn? If not inborn, is it possible, as well
might be, that they emerge, or at least reach dangerous propor-
tions, at the time of adolescence and its onset?

The bigger boys on the island are around twelve years old,
and the smaller around six years old, though there are all ages
in between. There is, that is to say, at least the beginning of
adolescence between the biguns and the littluns. Ralph, who
dreams earlier of 'the imagined but never fully realised place',
remembers, if he is not false to himself, a time, created in vivid
details (p. 107), when 'Mummy had still been with them and
Daddy had come home every day.' At that time, 'Everything
was alright; everything was good-humoured and friendly.' In
trying to account for 'things breaking up' on the island he seems
to be partly trying to account for the loss of that time. And yet
Ralph's feelings on the matter are ambivalent. He yearns always
for the apparent order of adulthood and he conceives himself
irrevocably embarked on the journey towards it:

'Then there were his nails—Ralph turned his hand over
and examined them. They were bitten down to the quick
though he could not remember when he had restarted this
habit nor any time when he indulged it.
"Be sucking my thumb next—" He looked round furtively.
Apparently no one had heard.'

This is one of many hints that those who look up to the adult
world they have lost also fear a regression to childhood which is
coming upon them. Ralph's ambiguous feelings to youth are
echoed all the way through. In one way the work looks back on
infancy as allied to paradise. In another it finds infancy and the
return to it as a return to prehistoric savagery by the individual.
The littluns' nightmares of a beastie are in fact more true than
a factually minded boy like Piggy can grasp. Ralph partly, and
Simon more fully, understand this. Jack understands it but turns
his back on it.

The littluns are contemptible because they can do so little except build castles and have diarrhoea, and yet they are, for Ralph at least, the cause of a mild jealousy because their lives are so relatively simple. The treatment of them by the author is guarded and interesting. 'They cried for their mothers much less often than might have been expected. They seldom bothered with the biguns and their passionately emotional and corporate life was their own' (p. 57). They played 'if not happily, at least with absorbed attention.'

We see this world 'at peace' invaded by members of the 'dubious region inhabited by Simon and Robert and Maurice', neither biguns nor littluns, but somewhere in between. Their behaviour is spontaneous and wantonly destructive:

> 'Roger led the way straight through the castles, kicking them over, burying the flowers, scattering the chosen stones. Maurice followed, laughing, and added to the destruction. The three littluns paused in their game and looked up. As it happened, the particular marks in which they were interested had not been touched, so they made no protest . . .'
>
> (p. 57).

Percival, one of the young ones, whimpers with an eye full of sand. Maurice is old enough to feel guilt and responsibility, though these are memories of imposed discipline, not inborn faculties:

> 'In his other life Maurice had received chastisement for filling a younger eye with sand. Now, though there was no parent to let fall a heavy hand, Maurice still felt the unease of wrongdoing. At the back of his mind formed the un-certain outlines of an excuse. He muttered something about a swim and broke into a trot'
>
> (p. 58).

Henry, the oldest of the three littluns present, 'was a bit of a leader this afternoon', and he goes off to observe the creatures of the shore. He pokes about with his stick, and there emerges in him in diminutive form what is discernibly the same urge as that which governs Jack:

> 'He became absorbed beyond mere happiness as he felt himself exercising control over living things. He talked to them, urging them, ordering them. Driven back by the tide, his footprints became bays in which they were trapped and gave him the illusion of mastery. He squatted on his hams at the water's edge . . . and the afternoon sun emptied down invisible arrows'
>
> (p. 59).

Meanwhile, Roger observes him, and he sees also Johnny 'crooning to himself and throwing sand at an imaginary Percival', who has done nothing that we know of to deserve such treatment, though he has an impossible name. Roger throws a stone at Henry, aiming to miss:

> 'Roger stopped, picked up a stone, aimed, and threw it at Henry—he threw to miss. The stone, that token of preposterous time, bounced five yards to Henry's right and fell in the water. Roger gathered a handful of stones and began to throw them. Yet there was a space round Henry, perhaps six yards in diameter, into which he dare not throw. Here, invisible, yet strong, was the taboo of the old life. Round the squatting child was the protection of parents and school and policemen and the law. Roger's arm was conditioned by civilisation that knew nothing of him and was in ruins'
>
> (p. 59).

Henry sees the stone and merely laughs, 'looking for the friend who was teasing him', taking it as no more than a game. It is a game, as we have seen, with possibilities.

Here, then, we have neither an idealised nor a totally pessimistic picture of childhood. What is plain is that the urge to destroy or to injure is already present, but it is not present clearly in a greater degree than in the older children and they do not, therefore, in any simple way, revert to childhood. Yet, the further back you go, the less you must find of that 'conditioning' which governs Maurice in a small degree and, on this occasion, Roger in a greater one. Conscience and responsibility are shown being developed, and they are not inborn but the product of that adult world which 'was in ruins'. Such 'conditioning' and conscious education are not, I think, criticised in themselves in the book, but for what they have become—the book does not claim that they must inevitably come to this, but that they have done so. We do not doubt, and Golding does not seem to doubt, that, despite its apparent arbitrariness and even its irrelevance to the island, the 'taboo of the old life' which prevents Roger from aiming at Henry is a good one. Without it, though, without the conditioning (or more nearly without it), and without the 'shame and self-consciousness' which go with it and from which Jack liberates himself by his war-paint, you have both the unrestrained drives and, to balance them, the absorbed games of the children (whatever their martial associations), their 'passionately emotional and corporate life', their ability to be 'at peace'. Moreover, if the taboo of the civilised world is so universal and in a limited way works for good, it is presumably no less instinctive than is the impulse to destroy, may indeed be inseparably part of that impulse.

But it is clear that, if the children may not be *responsible* for any destruction, they are certainly capable of causing it. Are Jack and his crew, though older, equally not responsible? They are, we are told, inspired by a leader who is possessed of a hunger to hunt and to dominate which is simply outside his own control. That it is so appears, indeed, to be a premise—it is not very profitable to argue that it *should* have been within his control. Morally perhaps it should have been but, factually, and very credibly, it simply wasn't.

This is, in fact, the familiar tension of works concerned with the Fall. One way or another, the power is built up to suggest that an action was inevitable. Reason tugs us always to believe that it was not so, that man is fully responsible. Either way his culpability cannot be explained but as divinely given, or the result of centuries of conditioning which have been found in many ways socially beneficial, even when society is depicted as inadequate as it is here.

For—and I do not think it is to deny the power of the book to say that it appears somewhat partial in its emphasis here—those drives to which the evil is most readily ascribed can work also for what we take to be good, for action and society of some sort which, however imperfect it may be, the children value and not merely in delusion. They are energies which can work for good or evil, but the choice, though it exists, is depicted as not entirely free. There is nothing particularly regrettable or censurable about the early experience of triumph; 'Eyes shining, mouths open, triumphant, they savoured the right of domination. They were lifted up. They were friends!' (p. 29). But this 'right of domination' cannot be distinguished categorically from those other dominations which issue less savourily in catastrophe. The domination of the human world, which may or may not of itself work for evil, stems gradually and indistinguishably from the domination of the animal world which is necessary for survival. The analogy between animal and human is always there; it is no accident that he is called Piggy and his body twitches when he dies like that of a dead pig.

If there is a 'loss of innocence' here it is, then, seen to be the loss of a relative innocence. There is no pure innocence presented, nothing to be presumed perfect. We are led to feel that, if there is no original fall conceivable by the imagination, the need for the myth of one is real, for no purely relative and repetitive version of the fall can make final sense.

*   *   *

How far is Golding creating myth in one sense, and how far is he using it, taking it over in another sense—'imposing a pattern', limiting but at the same time directing the implications of his art? This question throws us into a consideration of his very versatile style.

The schoolboys come from various backgrounds and perhaps from various types of school. It is to be expected, therefore, that they will not always use the same idiom. Their ways of speech are also governed by the situation in that they gradually abandon their more stereotyped idioms for a tenser manner appropriate to their condition, returning from time to time to 'school language' and showing us the gulf between them and the secure world of school.

But, though this is in the main a satisfactorily credible rather than a realistic fiction, there are points when their speech or their reactions strain, if they do not actually violate, credibility. Personal impression and opinion are the only guides. I doubt, myself, whether a likely early reaction is the repeated speculation that 'perhaps there aren't any grown-ups anywhere' (in these words). It is imaginable from six-year-olds, but not from Ralph who is twelve. It creeps in because of the very important parallel between the island and the adult world from which the children have been ejected and which they ambivalently reject. The temptation to ambiguity is also at times irresistible—it means also 'perhaps all adults are really children' playing with atom bombs instead of stones. Piggy, in his naiveté, credibly talks of 'my auntie', but again, in my experience, if a boy of this age dares to refer to his father among his mates, it is as 'my Dad', with a glorified account, rather than the cosy 'Daddy'. As for 'Mummy', she is a general taboo in schoolboy discourse. Again, boys do not, surely, in this number, divide into units the size of two tribes. They have had quite enough of 'houses' and 'tribes' officially, whatever security they may represent, and prefer 'gangs', a word not used. Jack's sadistic element is certainly credible; the only thing that is surprising is that, even considering those hints and suggestions we have noted, it is not far more widespread. Percival Wemys Madison, The Vicarage, Harcourt St Anthony, Hants., however, is entirely probable, and he might well talk of Mummy and Daddy, though, unless he is a new boy, one would have thought the others would have beaten him out of that by now. Piggy's speech, though it becomes rather a cliché by the end of the book, is also very acceptable, but is curiously confined to him—what is he doing in this school with its accents and names from elsewhere? The parachute affair has already been mentioned. Frankly, I do not think parachutes are or were so far from the minds of schoolboys as to excite this baffled wonder and for the chute to follow Simon out to the pre-natal sea is too much to ask.

These are minor criticisms, but many more such details could be added, for the effect of repeated detail here arouses some un-easiness as to the total effect. The crux of this is the part played by the style of the narrator. This is something introduced and developed by the author and with no parallel in *Coral Island*, where the strange bonhomie of the three boys and their ready optimism are all part of the author's tone and assumed by his spokesman Ralph the Rover, where also Jack is eighteen, Ralph fifteen, and the rest nearer the world of apprentices and sailors' mates than of younger schoolboys.

There are many points in *Lord of the Flies* where the narrator does not merely narrate but introduces brief comments to direct us towards the themes. The twins Sam and Eric, captured by Jack the tribal leader, protest 'O I say' and 'Honestly!' from 'out of the heart of civilisation'; 'civilisation' is an ironic word, associated with the (in this perspective) worthless orderliness of the naval cutter and its men, and with the atom bomb. Could the twins not have been allowed to speak for themselves?

Jack, having killed the pig (though he 'twitched' at the idea), 'sought in his charitable happiness to include them in the thing that had happened'; 'His mind was crowded with memories; memories of the knowledge that had come to them when they closed in on the struggling pig, knowledge that they had out-witted a living thing, imposed their will on it . . .' Jack's mind was plausibly so filled, but these are the words of the narrator and they do no more than repeat what has already appeared a sufficient possibility in the course of the action. Ralph's mind is certainly entering on the nostalgia and conflicts of adolescence, yet 'that imagined but never realised place' is surely a poetic concept too precisely intent on suggesting the nebulous. We have heard of what he feels he has lost, and we know that, much as he laments it, he also senses its inadequacy against some ideal inexpressible. There is no need to say more.

Simon has inclusive vision in advance of his 'middle' years. He has not, however, particularly in public, the ability to put it into words, and Golding has to do it for him. Thus 'However Simon thought of the beast, there rose before his sight the picture of a human at once heroic and sick', and he 'became inarticulate in his effort to express mankind's essential illness'.

But the crucial case is that of Simon and the narrator as describer. It is evident at our first extended acquaintance with Simon in Chapter Three that the easy and spacious, but precisely observant, style of the describer is closely associated with the vision of Simon. This is clear in the passage quoted above where fruit and flower grow on the same bough and Simon observes the advance of evening from his bower of creepers. This passage, about Simon's contemplation, is closely followed by another, hard to distinguish in style, where a mirage is recounted, and of course dismissed by the 'scientific' Piggy:

'Strange things happened at midday. The glittering sea rose up, moved apart in planes of blatant impossibility; the coral reef and the few, stunted palms that clung to the more elevated parts would float up into the sky, would quiver, be plucked apart, run like raindrops on a wire or be repeated as in an odd succession of mirrors. Sometimes land loomed where there was no land and flicked out like a bubble as the children watched . . . At midday the illusions merged into the sky and there the sun gazed down like an angry eye. Then, at the end of the afternoon, the mirage subsided and the horizon became level and blue and clipped as the sun declined. That was another time of comparative coolness but menaced by the coming of the dark. When the sun sank, darkness dropped on the island like an extinguisher and soon the shelters were full of restlessness, under the remote stars'

(p. 56).

This is not a vision observed by Simon, but purely the narrator's description. It is 'mystery' said to be 'ignored' by the boys, because they are accustomed to it (and only to Simon is the accustomed productive of fresh wonder). It is surely to be read, however, with the identical sympathy we accord to the contemplation of Simon.

The sea and the winds, which overcome Ralph but which Simon can satisfactorily grasp, point to an order, on the whole beneficent despite the storm, and certainly timeless, in which both the atomic and the island worlds are set; they are indeed logically part of that order, but one is given the feeling that they have fallen unaccountably away from it:

'Now he saw the landsman's view of the swell and it seemed like the breathing of some stupendous creature. Slowly the water sank among the rocks, revealing pink tables of granite, strange growths of coral, polyp, and weed. Down, down, the waters went, whispering like the wind among the heads of the forest. There was one flat rock there, spread like a table, and the waters sucking down on the four weedy sides made them seem like cliffs. Then the sleeping leviathan breathed out—the waters rose, the weed streamed, and the water boiled over the table rock with a roar. There was no sense of the passage of waves; only this minute-long fall and rise and fall'

(p. 101).

This is what Ralph sees, and he fears it as 'the divider, the barrier'. Simon, on the other hand, 'nodded' that indeed the sea was vast, but found the assurance that 'you'll get back where you came from'. And Simon himself indeed recognisably does so as 'softly, surrounded by a fringe of inquisitive bright creatures, itself a shape beneath the steadfast constellations, Simon's dead body moved out towards the open sea.'

I am less concerned with the evocative quality of this writing —it seems to me remarkable—than with its function in the novel as a whole. It seems to me quite clear that its function is thematic; it endorses the vision of Simon. In its comments too the narrator's style is close to the glimpse of man's 'essential illness' which Simon cannot articulate. The climax of these comments is at the end, with Ralph weeping 'for the end of innocence, the darkness of man's heart, and the fall through the air of the true, wise friend called Piggy'. It seems to me that we here experience an embarrassment which we have sensed intermittently before. What is to be done by the summing up is what has already been done by the descriptive style in previous passages, and what is done in those passages has already been done by the vision of Simon; there is an extravagance in this insurance policy method which runs a grave risk of making the whole conception appear grossly inflated.

We have already noted the fits and nervousness of Simon. The handicapped visionary is no literary innovation, but I do not recall another handicapped visionary schoolboy, and there seems to me in the idea an element of the ludicrous. When all justice has been done to the overall conception and the contribution of details in *Lord of the Flies* there is a disproportion in the work which the sailor's setting of the thing in perspective only partly and insufficiently acknowledges. The descriptive scenes suggest a theme alright, but are they not somewhat vast in implication and the portentousness emphasised by the partial identification with the vision of Simon? There is a richness here of tropical atmosphere and a linguistic intensity appropriate to the closing in of a claustrophobic pressure. But there is also the ever-present self-consciousness from which Jack and Ralph endeavour to escape. 'Darkness' and 'the delicate thing' (the conch) are ladled out too generously. Mad opaque gleams occur in more superficially sensational scenarios than this. The end of innocence and the darkness of man's heart are immensities whose vagueness is of an order different from the inarticulate sense of a broken world felt by Ralph, shattering as that may be to him. And Piggy, Ralph's friend truly enough, and in his eccentric manner 'wise' also, is not the type of true wise friends everywhere, but the one true wise friend (in his special and limited estimation) whom Ralph has so far come across. There is something here over-solemn, over-anxious to be universal in import, and I think this comes back to the conception of personal myth which is at work.

The concrete situation dramatically realised should have been enough, but was felt not to be. The presence of the comments (even in this work which seems to point to the inadequacy of comments)[9] suggests that this is so. There are the views of the three biguns and Simon on the nature of the beast, forming patterns which must, by Ralph, who attains some final insight, and by the reader who is invited to come to the same conclusions (granted his reaction to the sailor's disdain is fittingly ironic) be rejected. Even Simon dies with a very confused vision, in which conclusions as to the nature of the beast are hardly formed. He is crying about a man on the mountain, and he has been told that the beast is 'close to' and 'part of' them. But we do not know if this for him confirms his tentative speculation that 'maybe it's only us', and the fact that it is not 'only them' but equally civilisation as primitive man is not confirmed till Ralph finally weeps. Indeed, it is doubtful if it is confirmed there, or rather only in the reader. For even that the beast is internal, but real and seeking always external forms in which to manifest itself, is a limited 'proposition', part of the tissue in the revelatory technique. The personal myth is rather the very process of recognition of the limited worth of propositions, and the assumption that that process, inseparable as it is from the form and nature of the particular work, is significant and valuable.

The Fall cannot be identified as occurring in any individual or in a single critical action. It does not occur in any particular stage of mental or physical development. It does not, in the view of *The Inheritors* as here, occur at any particular stage of human evolution. For there is always the good potentiality to be set against the loss. Ralph, weeping at the end, is hopeless, but the reader is not so; he can even consider the possibility that, for all the tragedy, it has perhaps been a 'fortunate fall', producing a valuable fuller awareness in one human being. The Fall is not clearly transcended by a work of art (whether it be Sammy Mountjoy's drawing or Jocelyn's spire, sublimating a passion whose nature he had not realised) unless its nature is thereby faced. So the myth of literary art survives, not in the Romantic sense that art transcends the fallen and divided state, but in the sense that it alone can represent the painful progress from a delusion and short-sightedness to self-recognition and realisation of the mystery of one's predicament as a whole. This the 'message' without the art cannot do. Nor, possibly, can the art without the 'message' in sophisticated form.

NOTES

CHAPTER 1. A SURVEY

1. See *Oxford English Dictionary*, s.v. 'myth'.
2. See Maud Bodkin, *Archetypal Patterns in Poetry*, Oxford, 1963, E. Leach, *Genesis as Myth*, London, Jonathan Cape, 1969, and J. Armstrong, *The Paradise Myth*, Oxford, 1969, 5–7.
3. C. S. Lewis, *An Experiment in Criticism*, Cambridge, 1961, Chap. 5.
4. *Poems of Alexander Pope*, Twickenham Edition, Vol. iii, ed. Maynard Mack, Yale, 1950, lxiiiff.
5. Stephen Spender, *The Struggle of The Modern*, London, Hamish Hamilton, 1963, p. 26.
6. T. S. Eliot, 'The Metaphysical Poets', in *Selected Essays*, London, Faber & Faber, 1951.
7. T. E. Hulme, 'Romanticism and Classicism', *Speculations*, ed. Herbert Read, Routledge and Kegan Paul, 1960, and the discussion of this theme in the biography by A. R. Jones, *Life and opinions of Thomas Ernest Hulme*, London, Gollancz, 1960.

CHAPTER 2. *PARADISE LOST*

1. See A. Williams, *The Common Expositor*, N. Carolina, and also J. M. Evans, *Paradise Lost and the Genesis Tradition*, Oxford, 1968.
2. The commentators note the distinction; man is not now so obviously superior as in the image of God and woman is to obey him as of law, but the extent of his loss of the 'image' is of course highly debatable, and the different status of obedience is more easy to invoke than to define. Milton consistently cites St Paul as the source for his views on the obedience of women, which, though not unique by any means, are more forthright than those of his contemporaries. In *Tetrachordon* he allows exceptions to the general rule (obedience to the wisest); but this sorts awkwardly with the divine sentence, which seems to imply an arduous and even apparently unreasonable state of obedience as opposed to that which existed in Eden. 'Not but that particular exceptions may have place, if she exceed her husband in prudence and dexterity and he contentedly yield, for then a superior and more natural law comes in, that the wiser shall obey the less wise, whether male or female'. Did Milton seriously suppose that the man would then 'contentedly yield'—any more than the Royalists contentedly agreed that the rule of the Commonwealth was at that juncture superior in prudence to that of Charles?
3. See Williams, op. cit., 87ff.
4. For an interesting reading of the poem on this assumption, see S. E. Fish,

Surprised by Sin, London, Macmillan 1967. I think, however, that, whilst this reading is a helpful one intermittently, too great a consistency is argued for it—we need to assume too totally that the poet was able to hold consistently a pre-lapsarian view on to which his reader will only slowly and partially stumble. An alternative view is sketched in J. Armstrong, *The Paradise Myth*, Oxford, 1969, 111–12.

5. This notion was not peculiar to Milton's Eve—see Williams, op. cit., p. 121.

6. *Christian Doctrine*, xii; 'Under the head of Death in Scripture must be understood as comprehended all evils whatever.' Milton indeed permits many senses of 'death'. Physical death is a merciful release (XI, 61), and contrasted with the immortality Adam and Eve might or might not have had either by not eating the Tree of Knowledge, or by eating of the Tree of Life (IX, 94; III, 66–7; V, 496ff); this promise of immortality was subject to obedience, yet different from that which is promised to fallen man, subject to faith and obedience, in Michael's instruction. The obscurity remains and was much debated in the commentaries; but it is Satan (for his purposes) and Eve who accept the perverted argument that the serpent has not in a sense 'died', just as it is Satan who maintains that the beast has 'died' by putting on knowledge and man can do likewise (IX, 713–4). Sexual knowledge is often referred to as 'death' in the sixteenth and seventeenth centuries, but Milton has made it plain that this existed before the Fall.

7. For an excellent summary of Milton's procedure in handling the opposed systems, in discussion and in the structure of the poem, see H. Gardner, *A Reading of Paradise Lost*, Oxford, 1965, 50–2.

8. See Appendix II, s.v. Arianism. Milton is Arian in the *Christian Doctrine*, but the relationship of this doctrinally to *Paradise Lost* is arguable. To put the uncertainly construed 'begetting' or promoting of the Son on the day of the angels' Fall seems to have been Milton's invention, but in making it a sufficient cause for the angelic revolt he left the way open for an awkward relationship to the delegation of power, although that obscurity itself lessens any tendency to 'separate' Father and Son in our minds. (V, 602–15, III, 315–22).

9. For a treatment of the problems posed by the hubristic motive in Milton and its relation to the 'Satanic' interpretation (by which, loosely, Satan is 'hero'), see R. J. Werblovsky, *Lucifer and Prometheus, A Study of Milton's Satan*, London, Routledge and Kegan Paul, 1952. The common opinion of the commentators was that the Tree gave knowledge of evil and good, and not some superior knowledge thought undesirable for Adam and Eve to possess. Milton's Satan develops the idea beyond this, and Raphael's discussion in Book VI, which also does so, means that it is an idea suggested by the poem—not merely by Satan who can be rejected—which nonetheless avoids commitment to a view of the Tree's potency. See Appendix II, s.v. Trees.

10. In *Genesis*, Eve does not herself receive the command, but her repeating it to the serpent led to the assumption that Adam repeated it to her. Eve

expresses no surprise when Adam recounts the ban to her (IV, 423ff),
so she possibly knows of it already, though it is here that Satan learns of it,
and Eve's lack of interest may be significant. How much she knows of its
connection with limited knowledge, however, depends on how much
Adam told her after his instruction from Raphael, for he does not warn
her specifically about this in his speeches discussing their separation.

11. A. J. Waldock, *Paradise Lost and its Critics*, Cambridge Univ, 1947, pb.
ed. 1964, p. 56.

12. Of Milton's recent critics, Cleanth Brooks seems to me most responsive
to the human relationship of Adam and Eve; my own view of it in the
context of the poem, and of readership ancient and modern, does, however, differ considerably from his. See C. Brooks in *A Shaping Joy*, London,
Methuen, 1971, 349–66.

13. The fullest treatment of the awkwardness and inconsistency of the handling of God is W. Empson's *Milton's God*, Chatto & Windus, 1961. The
more random points in the same author's *Some Versions of Pastoral*, Chatto,
1950, seem to me more helpful in that they lead less totally to the conclusion that because God is unsatisfactory the poem must be a failure or
should be viewed as a warning against God's shifty dealings with man.
The interpretation of 'justifye the wayes of God to men' (I, 26) on the
basis of VIII, 226 ('inquire Gladly into the wayes of God with Man')
seems to me to give the right emphasis; the ways of God in general are
mysterious but of the ways of God to men we have at least some experience
and interest, and the attention is properly moved from a doctrinal tract
to an action representing interpreted experience.

14. See Note 6 above and Appendix II, s.v. Trees.

15. cf. *Christian Doctrine*, X: 'It was called the Tree of Knowledge of Good
and Evil, for since Adam tasted it, we know not only evil but we know
good only by means of evil.'
Areopagitica: 'Perhaps this is the doom that Adam fell into, of knowing
good and evil, that is to say of knowing good by evil.'

CHAPTER 3. THE OLD ENGLISH *GENESIS B*

1. See Introduction to *The Junius Manuscript*, ed. G. P. Krapp, New York,
1931. All quotations are from this edition. See also *The Later Genesis*,
ed. B. J. Timmer, Oxford, 1954.

2. See Appendix I. *Genesis A* (97–102) follows Origen's widespread belief
that man was only created after the angels had sinned. *Genesis B* does not
clearly describe the creation of man as a consequence of the Fall of the
Angels—lines can be adduced to support either view. The creation of the
angels is described in the pluperfect, to suggest that it occurred before
the Prohibition of the fruit, even though it follows it in the poem. Eve is
created at Adam's request (816–18), whereas *Genesis A* follows the Bible
more closely on this.
In *II Enoch*, the angels fell on the Second Day of Creation, before the
creation of man. Many medieval scholastics held that the angels and

Adam were created at the same time, and Augustine seems generally inclined to this view.

On the identification of serpent and Satan, and the general background to the Old English poem, see J. M. Evans, *Paradise Lost and the Genesis Tradition*, Oxford, 1968, chaps. 1–4 (and 75–6, 88).

3. Augustine maintained in *De Gen.* xiv that pride was the first sin and the angels fell through it rather than envy, but obviously in modern terms the two are hard to separate. Aelfric mentions that Satan's pride was in physical perfection (*Pref. to Genesis*, ed. S. J. Crawford, E.E.T.S. (o.s.), 160).

4. Translations are from C. W. Kennedy, *Early English Christian Poetry*, Oxford, 1952, pb. 1963.

5. See Appendix I and Note 2 above.

6. Satan is as bright as the stars (256) and evidently related to the Lucifer tradition (*Isaiah* xiv, 13. See Appendix I.) In *I Enoch*, Azazel (here the leader of the revolt) is referred to as 'the first star which had fallen from heaven' and a special place of punishment of fire and binding is reserved in the north-west for the 'stars which did not come forth at their appointed times'. Some cosmological myth seems to be mixed with the Fall of the Angels. Lucifer's abodes in heaven and hell are in the north, and originally they were not distinct (*II Enoch*, x).

7. See, for example, *II Enoch*. The binding of Satan may be influenced by the Harrowing of Hell, but it is a common feature of apocryphal accounts of the Fall of the Angels, where Satan is bound in hell to await a worse punishment on the Day of Judgement. *I Enoch* i, 9 probably governed the canonical passages in *X Jude* vi, *II Peter* v, 8, and *Revelation* xii, from which the patristic accounts derive.

8. The nature of the messenger's thanks is not entirely plain. 'Begra' (both) (725) may refer to his having suborned both Adam and Eve, or to his having fulfilled both of the wishes of Satan (403–8, 750–5), which here parallel the Fall of the Angels.

9. The Devil disguised as an angel and suggesting the injustice of God's arrangements was evidently no strange figure to the Old English writers, appearing also in Cynewulf's *Juliana* of the ninth century (derived from the *Acta S. Julianae*, sixth century). Theologians' work suggests that the idea was widely accepted; see Gregory in Migne, *Patrologia Latina*, 74 (col. 702) and 76 (col. 510), and Ambrose, making the link with the Fall, in Migne, 14 (col. 311). There is a link with the dream of an angel messenger in *Paradise Lost* V, 55.

10. In *Apocrypha and Pseudepigrapha of the Old Testament*, ed. R. N. Charles, Oxford, 1913, vol. ii.

11. See Appendix II, s.v. Trees.

12. For the earlier belief, possibly involved here, that Adam could see angels before the Fall, cf. *II Enoch*, and *Vita Adae et Evae*.

13. In *Jubilees* ix, xv (second century B.C.), they spend a period outside the Garden first, and are seven years in it before the Fall occurs.

CHAPTER 4. *THE FAERIE QUEENE*, BOOK 1.

1. *The History of the World*, Book 1, chap. iii, in *Works of Sir Walter Raleigh*, ii, ed. Oldys and Birch, Oxford, 1829, 65-75.
2. See Chapter 2, Note 1.
3. Select passages from these discussions are in *The Works of Edmund Spenser*, Variorum Edition, i, ed. C. G. Osgood and H. G. Lotspeich, Johns Hopkins, 1943.
4. The most comprehensive examination of irony and the poet's persona in the poem is in the discussion of Book II by H. Berger, *The Allegorial Temper*, Yale Studies in English, 1957, 137.
5. *The City of God*, Everyman translation, 1945, ii, pp. 43-4.
6. This is the conclusion of K. Neill, 'The Degradation of the Red Cross Knight', in *That Souveraine Light*, ed. D. C. Allen and W. R. Mueller, Baltimore, 1952, but I feel that it is an oversimplification. The same author's emphasis on the sensuality of the Red Cross Knight in his Fall seems to be excessive.
7. See above, Note 4. cf. C. S. Lewis, *English Literature in the Sixteenth Century*, Oxford, 1954, p. 392; 'There is no irony or ambiguity. Some now would deny the name of poetry to writing of which this must be admitted. Let us not dispute about the name.' Certainly the prevailing spirit seems to be 'narrative' and 'tranquil', rather than questioning or minute, but I think there is more of irony and qualification by detachment than Lewis admitted.
8. This has been most fully and brilliantly analysed by C. S. Lewis, *The Allegory of Love*, Oxford, 1938, pp. 324-6, 330-3.
9. The fact that the Red Cross Knight is to become a saint does not seem to me to imply any special doctrine of election, other than was in fact present in Protestant, Calvinist, and Roman Catholic alike—and indeed is more the result of artistic interest than necessarily of belief. He is referred to as 'the true Saint George' in Canto II, 12, but in a way which indicates at that moment being rather far from present sainthood. There is no further reference to this destiny until Canto X, and it is only when we have read the work several times that the idea that he is in any exceptional way predestined to sainthood begins to creep into our reading. In a rather similar way, whether or not the grace which Arthur in a loose way represents (as a knight 'blest' by 'grace') is dependent on or independent of the co-operation of the Red Cross Knight, which has been much debated, seems to me incapable of resolution. The controlling effect seems to be less of making a positive and active contribution at some stage than of gradually abandoning a frame of mind which constituted an impediment. A thorough study of Spenser's thought comes down on the side of his general orthodoxy (V. K. Whittaker, *The Religious Basis of Spenser's Thought*, Palo Alto, 1950), but Lewis's conclusion in *English Literature of the Sixteenth Century*, Oxford, 1954, p. 385, seems a fair one: 'I am not arguing that Spenser was not a Calvinist. A priori it is very likely that he was. But

his poetry is not written so as to enable us to pick out his beliefs in distinct separation from kindred beliefs . . .'

10. The obscurity here is not, of course, merely that of Spenser. See Appendix II, s.v. Trees. For the close association of the Tree of Life, and eating of it, with Christ and Christian victory, see J. M. Steadman, 'The Tree of Life Symbolism in *Paradise Regained*', *R.E.S.* (n.s.) xi, 1960, pp. 384–91. In *Revelation* xii, 2, the leaves of the Tree of Life were 'for the healing of nations', the Tree becoming the Lignum Vitae. The balm may also be influenced by tradition from the *Vita Adae et Evae* (xxxvi), where Adam, seized with pain near the end of his allotted spell, asks Eve and Seth to do penance near the Garden in the hope that God will send an angel with a drop of balm from the Tree of Life, to heal him. The well is a fountain of the Tigris, by which Satan gains entry to Eden in *Paradise Lost*, IX, 72–3.

11. See A. O. Lovejoy, 'Milton and the Paradox of the Fortunate Fall', *E.L.H.*, iv, 1937, pp. 161–79.

CHAPTER 5. ROMANTIC ATTITUDES

1. See Coleridge, *Poetical Works*, Oxford Standard Authors Edition, 1967, 285.

2. *Biographia Litteraria*, xiv. For a full discussion of the contributions of Wordsworth and Coleridge and their varying accounts of the origin and composition of the *Lyrical Ballads*, see *Lyrical Ballads*, ed. R. L. Brett and A. R. Jones, London, Methuen, 1963.

3. From his reading of Shelvocke's *A Voyage Round the World by the Way of the Great South Sea* (1726), in which is recounted the shooting by one of the crew of an albatross following the ship in a spell of bad weather.

4. *The Borderers*, in Wordsworth, *Poetical Works*, Oxford Standard Authors Edition, 1936, p. 54.

5. For a perceptive treatment of Coleridge's symbolism, see M. Suther, *The Dark Night of Samuel Taylor Coleridge*, New York, 1960, and, of its origins, J. B. Beer, *Coleridge the Visionary*, London, Chatto and Windus, 1959, chap. 2. For the conjunction of moon and mist or cloud, cf. *Lewti*, in *Poetical Works*, p. 253.

6. The 'setting' of the Mariner's tale is illuminatingly discussed in R. L. Brett, *Reason and Imagination*, Oxford, 1960.

7. For a discussion of the complex effect of this literary pastiche, see G. Watson, *Coleridge the Poet*, Routledge & Kegan Paul, 1966.

8. See *Poetical Works*, pp. 295–6.

9. Little of substance has been added since the monumental *The Road to Xanadu*, of J. Livingston Lowes, Boston, 1927.

10. H. House, *Coleridge*, The Clark Lectures, Oxford, 1951.

11. Collins's *Ode on the Poetical Character* also makes use of the Miltonic setting, and his 'poetical character' conforms generally to the 'enthusiast' poet of Coleridge's concluding lines.

12. See Chapter 1. See also the comprehensive study of the growth of the

'organic' critical theory in M. H. Abrams, The *Mirror and the Lamp*, New York, 1958, and R. Wellek and A. Warren, *Theory of Literature*, London, Jonathan Cape, 1949, Chaps. xii, xv.

13. Keats, Letter to George and Thomas Keats, Dec. 1817 (in which occurs the definition of 'negative capability').

14. On the composition of the *Immortality Ode* and Coleridge's *Dejection*, see M. Moorman, *William Wordsworth, The Early Years*, Oxford, 1957, pp. 527–33, and *The Later Years*, Oxford, 1965, pp. 19–24.

15. Letter to Benjamin Bailey, 22 Nov., 1817.

16. See the perceptive article by M. Quinn, 'The Objectivity of Keats's Ode to Autumn', *Critical Survey*, 1965, ii, 346ff.

17. *Poetical Works*, Oxford Standard Authors Edition, 1908, p. 46, ll.121–4.

18. Ibid., ll.241–7.

19. A full consideration of Keats's 'Apollo' symbolism is B. Blackstone, *The Consecrated Urn*, London, Longmans 1959.

20. Shelley's *Prometheus Unbound* obviously employs and refers to several forms of the Fall myth, but its central concern is less with the Fall than with release from the fallen state, and for my present purpose is of peripheral interest. In part, however, the release of Prometheus and his reunion with Asia consequent on an act of his own will corresponds to Shelley's assessment of the intellect's role in the creative act (which is to sustain consciously the inspired notes of the Aeolian Harp so as to produce 'not melody alone, but harmony'), and in this sense there is a connection between the artist's fall, with a glimpse of Eden, and Adam's state before and after the Fall. This, and the possibly divisive nature of intellectual speculation as opposed to imaginative vision, is a major theme of the Romantics and their successors.

Byron's versions of the myth are mainly of a cyclic nature, or a praise of Experience as opposed to delusory innocence (the paradise with Haidee in Don Juan), and are fully discussed in M. K. Joseph, *Byron the Poet*, London, Gollancz, 1964.

CHAPTER 6. *LORD OF THE FLIES*

1. T. S. Eliot, *Four Quartets*, 1944. *East Coker* II:

> 'There is, it seems to us,
> At best only a limited value
> In the knowledge derived from experience.
> The knowledge imposes a pattern, and falsifies,
> For the pattern is new in every moment
> And every moment is a new and shocking
> Valuation of all we have been.'

The opening of *Free Fall*, where Sammy Mountjoy announces the futility of his great knowledge, which he rejects, seems to me to owe a certain amount to the Eliot of *Prufrock* and *East Coker*, or at least to represent some parallel; 'I have hung all systems on the wall like a row of useless hats.

They do not fit. They come in from outside, they are suggested patterns.'
(Faber ed., 1961, 6).
2. 'The School of Giorgione', in *The Renaissance*. He said it of art, but the point stands, for all arts are intended.
3. W. Golding, 'In My Ark', in *The Hot Gates*, Faber and Faber, 1965, 105.
4. See below, and M. Kinkead-Weekes and I. Gregor, *William Golding, A Critical Study*, Faber, 1967, Chap. 1.
5. All references to *Lord of the Flies* are to the Faber hardback edition.
6. The nightmares of the 'snake-beast' correspond to the 'warning dreams' we have seen in *Paradise Lost* and *The Faerie Queene*, Book 1.
7. Golding records in his essay 'Fable' (*The Hot Gates*, 89) that 'the boys were below the age of overt sex, for I did not want to complicate the issue with that relative triviality'. One can, I suppose, see what he means.
8. cf. 'Fable': 'I believed then that man was sick—not exceptional man, but average man. I believed that the condition of man was to be a morally diseased creation and that the best job I could do at the time was to trace the connection between his diseased nature and the international mess he gets himself into . . . To many of you, this will seem trite, obvious, and familiar in theological terms. Man is a fallen being. He is gripped by original sin. His nature is sinful and his state perilous. I accept the theology and admit the triteness; but what is trite is true; and a truism can become more than a truism when it is a belief passionately held.'
9. cf. 'Fable', op. cit., 97. Golding has indicated his awareness of this conflict in the process of writing the book. 'The author becomes a spectator, appalled or delighted, but a spectator. At this moment, how can he be sure that he is keeping a relationship between the fable and the moralised world, when he is only conscious of one of them? I believe he cannot be sure. This experience, excellent for the novel which does not claim to be a parable, must surely lead to a distortion of the fable.'

APPENDIX I

The Fall of the Angels

The story of the Fall of the Angels is less familiar than that of the Fall of Man. It is also a complicated matter obscure in places. What follows is an outline of the myth and its connection with that of the Fall of Man.

Whenever the Fall of the Angels gained wide acceptance as a myth, it is not recorded in any developed form in canonical writings, but only in apocryphal books from about the second century B.C.[1] and in later Rabbinical and Patristic commentaries. The first and probably generative version is the brief introduction to *Genesis* VI (see below Appendix II, under *Genesis*). Here it is recorded that Yahweh, apparently incensed that the divine spirit might be permanently transmitted to man, expelled the 'sons of God' who had mingled with the 'daughters of men', and limited the life of men to 120 years. Verse 4 ('There were giants in those days') was subsequently understood to refer to the progeny of this weird and illicit union, and it is probable that the verse is misplaced in the text.

This rather primitive story has numerous analogues in comparative myth where sexual intercourse with a divine being is punishable by death. The tragic but heroic account of Gilgamesh, for example, is that of a being with a goddess mother and a human father, and the duality fatally works itself out in his life.

The *Genesis* VI account omits motivation altogether and has none of the strong moral undertones of *Genesis* III. But it must surely have originated in the same taboo of hubris and limitation of right human activity as was subsequently read into it and served to link it with the account of the human Fall.

Revelation XII (7ff), narrating a future war in heaven between

Michael and the dragon with his angels, in which the latter are cast out and the dragon is identified as Eve's serpent and Satan, draws in part on earlier apocryphal material (notably *I Enoch*) which elaborated the account in *Genesis* VI and was of course historical rather than visionary or futuristic in conception. *Isaiah* XIX (12) in which Lucifer was for long mistakenly identified with Satan (as he is in the apocryphal books, particularly *I Enoch*, XVIII) also contributed to the myth, as did the story of the Fall of the King of Tyrus, with its hubristic theme, in *Ezekiel* XXVIII (12ff).

The uncertainty of canonical references to the Fall of the Angels and related events is in part due to the history of the name Satan. None of the Old Testament uses of the word clearly refers to a single Devil, and all can be explained by the word's having originally meant merely 'accuser' or 'obstructor' in a general way. *II Enoch* preserves an intermediate stage by referring to 'satans' apparently as unspecific devils. Belial ('worthless one') and Satan referred in the first place to the same personage and Belial was even the commoner of the two names. In *Enoch* the rebel angels are variously led by Semjaza, Satanail, Azazel, or Jequon, and in Rabbinical writing a former archangel Sammael, not distinguished from Satan, tempts Eve and tries to establish an earthly kingdom to rival God's heavenly one. In *I Enoch* the serpent and the Devil (or this rebellious leader) are identified[2].

Adam, like Satan, is in the Old Testament a generic name, although *Genesis* treats almost of a dramatically conceived individual. The *Genesis* account of the Fall of Man, read by itself, is not obviously concerned to give an account of a supposed first act of sin; certainly it is equally or more concerned to give a representative account of what may be held to be repeatedly occurring in the life of man. But of course the context, where it is closely preceded by the account of the Creation, has always led to its being read in a supposedly historical way, and this reading was made by the apocryphal writers and subsequently by the Fathers.

The composite myth of the Fall of the Angels, as it eventually materialised, was made up of two diverse and all but incompatible elements. On the one hand the sequential or historical reading of *Genesis*, the attempt to reconcile *Genesis* III and *Genesis* VI, leads to the assumption that the Fall of the Angels must have followed the Fall of Man, since the daughters of Adam (understood as the first man) must clearly follow his creation and Fall. We cannot tell when the identification of the serpent of Eden with Satan the fallen angel was first accepted, but, once it was accepted, there arose on the other hand the notion that the Serpent/Satan tempted Eve because of his jealousy at the creation of man, jealousy and pride which are made the motive of the Fall of the Angels. In the *Vita Adae et Evae* (probably written in the first centuries A.D. and based on *II Enoch*) Satan explains how he was asked by Michael to worship the newly created man, and refused, for which he and his angels were thrown out of heaven. This tradition subsequently entered the *Koran* (*c.* A.D. 650) XV, and is the basis of many of our later literary versions. It is clear that this tradition presupposes that the Fall of the Angels preceded the Fall of Man (but not his creation), whereas that mentioned above assumes the reverse. The final thread in this tangled skein is the widespread assumption that the Creation of Man was effected to compensate God for the Fall of the Angels, which therefore preceded it and the Fall of Man.

Despite its many inconsistencies, *II Enoch* (probably of the first century A.D.) gives us some idea of how a more or less unified account was constructed out of these diverse elements. There was a class of angels known as Grigori, the Watchers. Among them was a group of 'satans', led by Satanail, who rebelled against God before the 'daughters of men' affair. The guilt of the Watchers lay in becoming subject to the satans, a class with whom those who succumbed were later confusingly identified, although some of their number remained faithful. On the second day of Creation Satanail, with his angels, turned against God (for an unstated reason) and wished to place his throne 'higher than the clouds' and on a level with the throne of God. For this act of hubris the satans were all cast out of the fifth heaven and tortured and imprisoned in the second heaven. Some of them, however, went further, descended to earth, and mingled with the daughters of men. From this misalliance were born the giants of *Genesis* VI, 4. These angels were then imprisoned under the earth. The devils who afflict fallen men, however, were not these angels, but the misconceived spirits which came from the giants when God destroyed them. At some time unspecified in relation to these events, when man was created Satan envied him and wished to establish a hostile kingdom on earth. Out of envy he tempted Eve and secured her Fall.

Here, then, the various motivations for the malignity of Satan, and the diverse hints of a Fall of the Angels, are assimilated into a rough sequence of events, where the misalliance between angels and men, and the temptation of Adam and Eve, are separate consequences of an ambitious war in heaven. Once it is felt that there is a more than accidental connection between *Genesis* III and *Genesis* VI (as it *was* felt from early times), the reasons for the composite story are not hard to perceive.

To assert that the angels fell, even if it is only to push the problem one stage further back, is to deny that evil always co-existed with good, particularly on earth, and was created so, as Augustine argues against the 'pestilential sect' of the Manichees in *De Civitate Dei* (XI). It is a step towards exculpating God. Although of course a Fall of the Angels does not really bring us any nearer to a satisfactory explanation of the origin of evil, of how it affected the angels and later affected man, although Satan does not feature in *Genesis* and is only later identified with the serpent, and although free will rather than Satan's inherent evil is blamed for his and man's Falls—despite these considerations, the presence of an evil angel in the form of the serpent in later versions does superficially appear to be more comprehensible after supplying such a pre-history, and so the two-or-three stories are widely linked. Thus Augustine handles the issue of free will, and dismisses the notion that God ever created evil, first in the Fall of the Angels and then in the case of Adam and Eve (*De Civitate Dei*, XIII, XIV). By his time, the account of Adam's Fall, whether or not it represents a typical and recurrent situation, was viewed as unquestionably representing the *first* human sin, effectively caused by his free will, but made possible by the pre-existing evil of Satan curiously at large in the Garden.[3]

NOTES

1. The apocryphal works referred to are most conveniently found in *Apocrypha and Pseudepigrapha* of the Old Testament (ed. R. H. Charles, Oxford, 1913, Vol. ii).

2. *I Enoch* is a composite work of various dates and traditions, the extant version being of the first or second century B.C. It had some influence on the New Testament—particularly on *Revelation*—and was accepted by many of the early writers as canonical, though not by Augustine.

3. For an anthropologist's view of the recurrent story-patterns in accounts of the Creation and Fall, see E. Leach, *Genesis as Myth*, London, Jonathan Cape, 1969.

Terms and Facts Relating to the Fall Myth

Arianism. A heresy originated by Arius (*c.* 320) and refuted by the Council of Nicea (325) and the resulting Nicene Creed. The argument was an extension of the scriptural Father and Son, which asserted the separateness of God and Christ. Arius took his stand on the uniqueness of God and held that whatever exists apart from God must have been created by Him, not from Him but from nothing ('ex nihilo'). Therefore the scriptural 'beget' for the relations of Father and Son must be figurative, meaning merely 'make' (Milton's use of 'beget' in the arguments of Satan comes to mind). Christ is a perfect creature, not to be compared with others, but nonetheless a creature, not self-created or self-existent. It was through his agency—and this was why he was made—that the transcendent God could create the contingent earthly world.

Anglican Doctrine. The contemporary Anglican doctrine is by no means agreed. The strict historical belief is in *Article* IX (1662); 'Original Sin standeth not in the following of Adam (as the Pelagians do vainly talk) but it is the fault and corruption of the Nature of every man, that naturally is engendered of the off-spring of Adam; whereby man is very far gone from original righteousness, and is of his own nature inclined to evil, so that the flesh lusteth always contrary to the spirit . . .' This, and the explicit identification with 'concupiscence and lust' which follows, would no doubt not be accepted by many practising Christians today, but its tradition is apparent in literary works concerned with the Fall.

Aquinas (1225–74). For Aquinas, Original Sin is the absence or deprivation of 'original righteousness', whilst the 'pura naturalia' of man remains unimpaired, for, to Aquinas, man's Fall was from a state of 'supernature' to 'nature'. Like Augustine, he regards 'concupiscence' as the 'matter', and the lack of 'original righteousness' as the 'form', of Original Sin, but he revives the conception of a Limbo and is generally less austere and rigid than Augustine. Adam is responsible for the 'seminal identity' of his descendants; sin is conveyed at birth, whether or not it is in fact communicated by the sexual act itself.

Augustine (354–430). The shape of Augustine's thought had a good deal to do with his early adherence to the Manicheans and was formed long before the Pelagian controversy. With some hesitation, he supports a literal and historical reading of *Genesis* III, but he greatly develops the notion of the Garden as a state of 'original righteousness', which is scarcely more than latent in the Biblical version, and thus plays no small part in establishing the tradition of a glorious pastoral and moral pre-lapsarian state on which literary versions expatiate.

Augustine distinguishes between the 'reatus' of sin (a responsibility for Adam's transgression which still rests on all his posterity by reason of their 'seminal identity' with him), and the 'vitium', which consists of 'concupiscence', evil in itself, transmitted by and in parentage. Neither of these conceptions appears very acceptable to the modern mind, but the influence of both, and the stringent asceticism which they led him to advance, are of incalculable importance.

Sombre as is Augustine's view of man as a 'mass of sin', degenerate both by his responsibility for the first sin and by his constant propensity to re-enact it, it stops short of total depravity or determinism. Nonetheless, it moved near enough these extremes—holding that the unbaptised who have committed no sin of their own are, by virtue of their solidarity with the original sin of Adam, liable to hell—to be at the centre of the Pelagian controversy when it developed.

The strongly positive element in Augustine's thought, the

doctrine of grace, is exceedingly hard to summarise, both because of the complexity of his arguments and because his views are not always consistent. Man is generally passive in the reception of grace and has no power to aid or impede it, yet it seems to be Augustine's teaching that this gift of grace implants afresh in man the power of free will so that he is again capable of choosing good. One of the most profound, but one of the most baffling, elements of his thought is this constant close association of free will and determinism.

Augustine is consistent in placing the blame for the Fall on Adam's (and man's) misuse of free will and considers that pride and a desire for independence played a large part in this error. 'Concupiscence' is strictly for him a distraction from divine things, but sexuality appears to him to be the chief distraction, and, if he does not equate sexual passion and original sin, he is certainly at pains to stress their intimate connection.

Prominent in his thought is the difficult conception that God's prescience, which is absolute, is not an effective limitation of his gift of free will. His involved arguments on this problem couple with his insistence that the elect are chosen for eternity and limited in number to those needed to replace the fallen angels to suggest a somewhat deterministic bias.

Fall of the Angels See Appendix I.

Genesis The history of the *Book of Genesis* and its composition is of considerable uncertainty. It is, however, generally held that the book is a composite work made up of three or more strands of narrative composed at different times. There are, as a result, at least two accounts of the myth in it.

The main and basic account is in Chapters II and III, but some elements of this version (notably the rivers in Eden and semi-Promethean matter in III, xxii–iv) seem to be of different date and traditions. For the obscurity of the two Trees, see below.

It will be noted that there is in the main account no mention of the Fall of the Angels, that the serpent is not identified with

Satan, that man is not specifically said to be endowed with immortality or any particular nobility, and that he is put into the Garden to work and not to luxuriate. There is the matter of 'enmity' and bruising of heads, but on the whole the Old Testament and Gospels offer the facts and the sense of sin which the idea of Original Sin was formulated to explain, but they do not offer the idea itself in a formal way. It is not until St Paul that there is a fairly clear linking of man's apparently fallen state with the sin of Adam, although some idea of Original Sin is known to have been held by the Jewish Church at the time of Christ. In fact, the idea of a Fall was arrived at from a priori reasoning, and then the 'evidence' for it produced from canonical writings.

This 'evidence', although by the time of St Paul the Adamic story was invoked, was at first rather the other account, in *Genesis* VI, 1–4. These verses are in no clear relation to the story of Adam and indeed in manner they amount almost to a new start to the book. The account of the envy of God for the daughters of men, the confusion of divine and human and the resulting miscegenation is, elaborated in the apocryphal *Books of Enoch* and played some part in the stress on sexuality in the idea of Original Sin—a stress very easily superimposed on the Adamic account.

The Fall of the Angels is not, as has been said, a part of the early accounts, though it is related to that in *Genesis* VI, but the brief version in *Revelation* XII (7–11) identifies Satan and the serpent, follows it with the attribution of future victory to Christ, and thus plays a considerable part in the development of the whole Christian cycle (see Appendix I).

Manichaeism. Manes (*c.* 215–276) was the founder of a sect whose beliefs are hard to define and which seem almost a separate religion rather than an unorthodox form of Christianity. Augustine, for some time a Manichean, was the chief source of his ideas in the West.

The essential Manichean belief was the eternal coexistence of the opposed principles of good and evil, each dependent for its existence on the other, and the faith laid much weight on the intellectual and moral progress of the individual—it was a severe and ascetic creed. Good and evil were seen to be light and dark respectively and this association went beyond the metaphorical in that no clear distinction was made between the ethical and the physical, so that redemption was a deliverance of fractions of light from darkness. To the Manicheans evil was inseparably associated with darkness and matter, and it was man's obligation to free himself as far as possible from the matter in which he appeared tragically lost, and to make of himself the particle of light which he could be.

In the Romantic period individualism and introspection often combine with a gloomy reaction to earthly life, which is seen as a darkness opposed to an ideal sphere of light, to suggest what can be called a Manichean view of things, but here, of course, the details of Manichean discipline and the dogmatic moral approach were not at all observed.

Origen. Origen is chiefly important for his theory of pre-existence, which was of a Platonic nature. He does not accept the story of the Creation and the Fall except as a cosmic myth and symbol. In his view there existed before the creation of the world all the souls, rational essences, which ever would exist. They were all equal and endowed with free will but, with the exception of Christ, they opted to fall away from God. The result was a forefeiture of equality and a transference into material bodies. Their fallen state is a temporary one, though they may undergo many reincarnations before they are restored to their first condition.

Of such a Fall, Adam is taken as symbolic, illustrating both the original fall of the essences and the subsequent fall of other souls. The clothes which Adam and Eve make are, for instance, regarded as representing bodily existence, which, however, Origen does not regard as intrinsically bad.

Paradise. The old Persian word, adopted also by Hebrew, Aramaic, and Greek, signifies simply a 'Garden' or 'park' and such paradises are usually tended and shaped by man. Thus the Miltonic Paradise of Eden is essentially a walled garden and the tilling of it is a realising of its full potential. The word is used generally of gardens in the Old Testament, but exclusively of Eden in *Genesis* II–III, and of the afterworld for the righteous when it appears in the New Testament. In the apocryphal *Enoch* and *Ezra*, these two conceptions, formerly distinct, are identified, and the identification became common Jewish belief shortly before the birth of Christ. At an intermediate stage 'Paradise' was also used of the abode for the righteous after death but before resurrection. There is some uncertainty as to which conception Christ refers to in 'Today shalt thou be with me in Paradise' (*Luke* XXIII, 43) for beliefs were at this time in a state of transition.

The root of the word 'Eden' is disputed, the alternatives being 'wilderness of plain' or 'delight', the second of which fosters the identification with Paradise after death. The four rivers of Eden, in *Genesis* II, 10–14, seem to be an accretion to the main account of the Garden, and only two of them, the Tigris and the Euphrates, have been identified. These two, however, can hardly have been thought of as springing from a common source and suggest rather that the whole conception is to be taken symbolically as implying that Eden was the centre of the known world.

In comparable myths the Garden is first God's private park into which, after a certain period, he puts other beings.

St Paul. For practical purposes the doctrine of Original Sin has its start in the unspecific connection made by St Paul between Adam and mankind in general (*I Corinthians* XV, 22, and *Romans* V, 13–17). The question of man's solidarity with Adam— his notional participation in and responsibility for the first sin— is not discussed by St Paul; it is Adam as a symbolic and representative being of all time which seems to concern him. It has been thought that his references are of so parenthetical a nature that they must represent doctrine commonly accepted whilst he was alive, but, however this may be, the *Epistles* seem to have been considerably responsible for the emphasis on the Adam story, as opposed to that in *Genesis* VI, in the early Church.

The two disasters consequent to the Fall were, in St Paul's view, mortality and a propensity to sin. This inheritance is closely associated with the body and there is some parallel between St Paul and St Augustine in the urgency of their warnings against 'concupiscence', which St Paul regarded as a prime factor in the Adamic story (*I Timothy*, II, 9–15).

Pelagianism. Pelagius (*c.* 400) denied both the transmission of a fault or corruption from Adam, the descendants' responsibility or participation in the first sin, and also the necessity of a directly assisting grace. Pelagius is the exponent of free will *par excellence.* The Fall of Man he regarded as symbolic of what had been and might be enacted—the only connection between it and Adam's descendants is that of example and parallel. Pelagius did not accept that the propensity to sin is propagated in sexual love and he held that infants are born in a state of total innocence. The view that in some way man cannot avoid sinning he held to be an insult to man and to his Creator. Free will he held to be a supreme gift from God and reward or punishment depended on its proper exercise.

Roman Doctrine. Council of Trent (1545–63). The Original Righteousness, which was lost at the Fall, was an addition, a 'donum superadditum', rather than man's nature, and his actual nature, his 'pura naturalia', was weakened rather than immutably depraved by the Fall. Sin is conceived of as voluntary and 'concupiscence', though a consequence of the Fall, is not strictly or solely of the nature of sin. But Original Sin is, in an undefined way, transmitted by physical generation. Free will was limited, not destroyed, by the Fall, and grace is necessary to salvation.

Trees of Life and Knowledge. The Tree of Life only plays a significant role in the *Genesis* story after the Fall, where man is prevented from gaining immortality through it (III, 22), and it is possible that this verse is an addition to an earlier account. But, although the Tree of Life is from the first 'in the midst of the garden', it is on the Tree of Knowledge that the ban is placed and no ban on the Tree of Life is mentioned before the Fall. Yet, if there was no ban on eating this Tree, we must wonder why Adam was not already immortal (as II, 22, 24, suggest that he was not). This is an old conundrum, and the best that can be made of it is that immortality was forfeited either as a fact or as a prospect by the Fall; it was in some way more qualified than it was before.

In the account of the Fall itself there is mentioned only the 'Tree which is in the midst of the garden' and this is evidently the banned Tree, of the knowledge of good and evil, eating of which will cause death. (It was not, of course, an apple tree— the 'apple' probably arises from confusion of 'malus' (bad) with 'malum' (apple).) Whether, or in what sense, it might also cause knowledge was much debated. If 'knowledge of good and evil' refers to moral judgement, then Adam and Eve can hardly have been guilty of disobedience freely without such knowledge or acquired it afterwards. If it refers to wider secular knowledge, these acquisitions were made rather by their descendants (IV, 20ff). Self-consciousness, shame, and sexual knowledge may be found as the consequences of eating the fruit, but to make of them exclusively the 'knowledge' referred to seems to narrow the story beyond its effect.

The presence of life-giving trees and plants is well established in comparative myth and religion, but the writers of *Genesis* seem to be interested in the ban more as an example of obedience than as an example of the Promethean theme, and this and other elements, though much developed later, are hardly more than latent in *Genesis*. The historic association of 'knowledge' and 'death' with sexuality—indeed, the puns on these words in many languages—suggest that what was acquired by eating the fruit was a knowledge of the transience and conflicts of mortal existence and that the Tree of Life may have been incorporated, without much regard for strict consistency, because of its traditional status as a symbol of the difference between divine and human existence. But the fact is that only the vaguest of sense can be made of the Trees as they occur in the biblical story.

Index

Index

Index